CAMBRIDGE IGCSE ENGLISH WRITING

A COMPREHENSIVE GUIDE (FOR PAPER 1 AND PAPER 2
COURSE CODES: 0500,0990)

Dr. Jyuthica. K. Laghate

Clever Fox®
PUBLISHING

Chennai • Bangalore

CLEVER FOX PUBLISHING
Chennai, India

Published by CLEVER FOX PUBLISHING 2025
Copyright © Dr. Jyuthica .K.Laghate 2025

All Rights Reserved.
ISBN: 978-93-67073-13-1

This book has been published with all reasonable efforts taken to make the material error-free after the consent of the author. No part of this book shall be used, reproduced in any manner whatsoever without written permission from the author, except in the case of brief quotations embodied in critical articles and reviews.

The Author of this book is solely responsible and liable for its content including but not limited to the views, representations, descriptions, statements, information, opinions and references ["Content"]. The Content of this book shall not constitute or be construed or deemed to reflect the opinion or expression of the Publisher or Editor. Neither the Publisher nor Editor endorse or approve the Content of this book or guarantee the reliability, accuracy or completeness of the Content published herein and do not make any representations or warranties of any kind, express or implied, including but not limited to the implied warranties of merchantability, fitness for a particular purpose. The Publisher and Editor shall not be liable whatsoever for any errors, omissions, whether such errors or omissions result from negligence, accident, or any other cause or claims for loss or damages of any kind, including without limitation, indirect or consequential loss or damage arising out of use, inability to use, or about the reliability, accuracy or sufficiency of the information contained in this book.

CONTENTS

Preface .... *v*

1. Introduction 1

2. Directed Writing 5

3. Summary Writing 8

4. Letter Writing 14

5. Diary Entry and Journal Writing 23

6. Speech Writing 34

7. Interview Writing 41

8. Article Writing 47

9. Writing A News Report and A Formal Report 54

10. Writers Effect 64

11. Descriptive Writing 68

12. Narrative Writing 78

Author Biography: 86

iii

PREFACE

Cambridge IGCSE, English as First Language courses, (Course codes- 0500, 0990), entail an extensive focus on writing competencies. Fundamentally, from Key Stage 2 itself, elaborate writing exercises are incorporated and encouraged intensively in the curriculum.

The writing tasks are diverse and involve a directed or an instructional writing component and a major composition part consisting of narrative writing and descriptive writing.

This book is a comprehensive and specialised guide aiming to simplify all forms of writing asked in the examinations as well as assist students completely and appropriately to understand the entire planning, organisation and execution of various writing pieces in the most effective and timely manner.

It won't be an overstatement to state that the curriculum expects a solid writing acumen from the candidates and in a way develops key writing skills and facilitates a deeper understanding and nuances of analysis and crafting an excellent piece.

The process of developing writing effectiveness and flair is certainly complex and demanding for students since it is not as clear cut as mathematics.

To cater to these paramount issues, this book is written using an exam friendly and performance enhancement approach detailing each and every salient point of various forms of writing prompts asked according to the syllabus.

I sincerely hope that you all will be able to utilise this guide to the fullest and achieve your dream score.

Kind Regards,

Dr. Jyuthica.K. Laghate
Founder.Dr.J's Knowledge Café
Email:jyuths@gmail.com
Mobile: +917447789343

CHAPTER 1

INTRODUCTION

*P*aper 1 in the courses, namely, Cambridge IGCSE (0500) and Cambridge (9-1) IGCSE (0990) have long questions based on **writer's effect, a summary question and a persuasive writing task.**

The **total duration** of the examination is **2 hours**.

The writer's effect question is targeted at highlighting the **three powerful phrases or words** that have been employed by the writer in the selected two paragraphs of the extract to **create the intended effect** and **convey the meaning impactfully to the audience**.

The **writer's effect question** is a **15 marks** question with a **word limit of 200-300 words**. The candidate has to select three powerful words or phrases each from two paragraphs. The main intent is to write elaborately about how the author has used these words/phrases inorder to put forth the meaning and the desirable effect on the reader. **The various language techniques and devices used in the particular excerpts have to be analysed and the explicit and implicit meanings have to be understood and expressed**.

Summary question in Paper 1 is a **concise** summary of just **120 words** in IGCSE **(0500)** and IGCSE **(9-1-0990)** courses. It is a 15 marks question too.

The primary objective is to focus on what is asked and present the essential information in a precise manner. **Persuasive writing task** in Paper 1 is a 25 marks task with a higher word limit of **250-350 words.**

The types of persuasive writing types posed in the exam are:

1. Letters
2. Magazine Articles
3. News Articles
4. News Reports

5. Formal Reports
6. Interviews/ Podcasts
7. Speeches /Talks
8. Diary entry
9. Journal entry

This is a task based on the third passage or text in the Paper 1 exam and is based on specific directions or bullet points to be focused upon.

Paper 2 in various Cambridge IGCSE examinations like Cambridge IGCSE First Language English-**0500**, Cambridge IGCSE (9-1)-**0990** and Cambridge IGCSE (9-1), UK only -**0627** comprises of the first section dedicated to **Directed Writing** and the second section dedicated to **Composition** containing **Narrative writing and Descriptive writing**.

The **total duration** of the paper is **2 hours as well.**

Section A contains **one long form directed writing question** carrying **40 marks** and is based on **texts A and B** in Section A. 15 marks are reserved for the writing content and 25 marks are for the writing quality.

The word limit of this task is about **250-350 words** and involves reading, evaluating and extracting information from these two passages to craft a structured piece of writing. These pieces of writing can be persuasive such as **letter/speech/talk/interview/report/article/podcast and diary entry or a journal entry.**

Section B consists of Question numbers 2,3,4,5 which are two descriptive and two narrative writing prompts. **Out of these four tasks, the candidate is provided with the option to write on any one task**. The advantageous part of this question is that there are a lot of options and one can choose according to their strength **whether it is narrative or descriptive writing. Composition is a 350-450 word task**.

The principal writing assessment objectives in Section A and Section B as prescribed in the Cambridge IGCSE 2023 syllabus are as follows: (Source – 596961-2023-syllabus.pdf (cambridgeinternational.org))

Introduction

1. Express what is **thought, felt and imagined**.
2. **Organise and convey facts, ideas and opinions effectively**.
3. Demonstrate a **varied vocabulary** appropriate to the context.
4. Demonstrate an **effective use of sentence structures.**
5. Demonstrate an understanding of **audience, purpose and form.**
6. Demonstrate accuracy in **spelling, punctuation and grammar**.

One of the most vital things to facilitate a good performance is effective time management as well as planning and organising data according to the type of the question.

The time devoted to the questions should be based primarily according to the length of the expected answer. For example, in Paper 2, Narrative and Descriptive writing task is a longer task (350-450 words). So, ideally more time should be dedicated to it.

Before venturing into any types of writing in IGCSE Paper 1 or Paper 2 whether it is a summary, writers effect or persuasive writing it is important to plan your writing based on the following cardinal points:

1. **What is the message that you want to give?** – Messages can be direct or explicit messages present in the extracts or implicit or indirect messages that you can provide as a part of your opinion or view especially in persuasive writing.

2. **How you are going to deliver the content?** - For different writing types, there are different tenets to be kept in mind. For instance,

   I. For summary, the language needs to be factual, not very flowery, exactly answering the question and mentioning all the relevant points.
   II. For writer's effect, the student should convey what is the intended meaning of the powerful words/phrases, how the author has used language devices to create an impact and what has been the effect of the word/phrase choices.
   III. As far as letter is concerned, it is important to annotate the points given in the passages, paraphrase and present a suitable introduction and conclusion.

IV. In terms of writing a powerful magazine or newspaper article, the tone should be assertive, catchy and supported by facts, opinions and evidence. Powerful usage of vocabulary in the form of relevant adjectives, adverbs, verbs, nouns and connectors is ideal.

V. In order to craft a brilliant news report, it is important to report or present when, what, where and how a particular event happened with impactful headline and a slightly dramatic language tone.

VI. For conversational pieces like speech, interview, talk or a podcast, it is important not be over formal in terms of language tone. The writing must be relatable, involving the target person or audience with interesting use of vocabulary, exclamations, idioms or sayings and engaging portrayal of experiences.

3. What is the target audience? Your language style, tone and structure should vary according to the target audience.

To exemplify,

I. To deliver a speech to young students, it would be unfruitful to use lot of jargons or very complex arguments. Rather, the speech needs to be appealing yet very conversational and simple.

II. While writing descriptive writing, it is crucial to use exaggerated tone, figurative devices and dramatic style to portray what you saw, heard, felt, smelled or tasted.

III. While presenting a compelling story, it is important to have rich description of characters, a gripping plot and a stellar climax and conclusion.

CHAPTER 2

DIRECTED WRITING

Directed writing or writing based on deriving information from the passages is asked as a compulsory question in both Paper 1 and Paper 2. The difference is that in Paper 1, it is based on one text and in Paper 2 it is based on two texts. The total word count for directed writing is about 250-350 words for both papers. However, the question carries 25 marks in Paper 1 whereas it carries 40 marks in Paper 2. Directed writing mainly focuses on persuasive writing skills and various types of persuasive writing are posed such as letter, speech, interview, talk, podcast, news report, general report, news article, magazine article, diary entry and journal entry.

It is very crucial and prudent to note that there are distinct differences in style, tone and structure of writing in these pieces and therefore having a detailed know-how of all these forms of writing is paramount to ensure excellence in the examination.

It is first vital to understand the foundations of persuasive writing since all these variants need to incorporate the essentials of persuasive writing.

As the name suggests, Persuasive Writing, aims to convince the reader and create a stronger impact, appeal or present a powerful argument.

Some of the crucial tools in drafting a persuasive master piece are:

1. A persuasive piece needs to have a powerful or assertive tone. Hence impactful adjectives, verbs, adverbs and nouns need to be employed.
   For e.g., Instead of using very common words such as 'important', adjectives such as 'paramount' or 'crucial' can be used. Employing adverbs is the key to portray the intensity of the verbs or adjectives such as highly, extremely, incidentally etc.
2. Simple verbs can be converted to potent nouns, a process called as 'nominalisation'. For e.g., instead of the verb 'destroy', the noun 'mass destruction' conveys the message cogently.

3. Appropriate connectors are very important to create either parallel arguments or contrast. For instance,

   Connectors such as However, Despite, Though, Although, Even though, Yet, But etc. can be used to indicate contrast.

   Connectors such as Similarly, Also, Additionally etc. can be used to indicate similar or parallel ideas.

   Connectors such as 'In a nutshell', 'Conclusively', 'To conclude', 'To infer', 'After careful consideration', 'In short' etc. can be used to start conclusion.

4. Hyperbole or Exaggeration can be utilised effectively to make the piece more impactful. For example, while writing about the after effects of global warming, it can be mentioned: Are we not abusing Mother Earth for ages and still expecting her to be compassionate?

5. Exclamations are important to convey the right emotion of shock, disgust and surprise especially for types like articles, speech, talk and interviews.

6. Rhetorical questions are highly beneficial to engage the reader and can be used at the start or end of the persuasive piece.

7. Two mnemonics that can be used to remember the persuasive devices are:

A FOREST and PERSUADER

A FOREST is an Acronym for:

   A- Alliteration, Adjectives but also Adverbs

   F- Facts and also Fallacies of the other party (Mainly for Argumentative pieces)

   O- Opinions

   R- Rule of Three (Repetition of the same word / phrase thrice)

   E- Emotive Language

   S- Statistics

   T- Talking to the reader

The other mnemonic is **PERSUADER** which is useful and applied mainly for argumentative articles, speeches, winning over an opposition, debate etc.

   P – Pronouns – Use of personal pronouns like You, We, Us etc. to engage the audience and make them feel valued.

E-Emotive Language to hook the audience

R- Repetition of words or phrases for impact

S- Statistics to back your statements with reliable data or evidence

U- Undermining the opposition by presenting conflicting arguments/proof

A- Anecdotes from experts adding more realism to the piece

D- Direct address to the audience improving the reach and appeal of the content

E- Exaggeration in moderation works wonders in a persuasive piece

R- Rhetorical Questions to compel the audience to think and relate closely with the material.

8. Some of the other three principles that are followed to produce an appealing persuasive write-up are:

Ethos

Logos

Pathos

Ethos is essentially appealing to the moral fabric of people and getting their trust.

E.g. - *Time has come when we need to respect individuals from all walks of life and not discriminate based on age, gender, ethnicity or socioeconomic status.*

Pathos is appealing to the emotions or suffering of people and generating a lot of sentiments in them such as sadness, feeling traumatised, guilty, alarmed etc.

E.g. – *The perils of COVID-19 are still fresh in our mind and therefore it needs to be like a long lasting campaign to adopt solid preventive measures.*

Logos as the name suggests is use of logical reasoning, facts and evidence to appeal to the reader.

E.g. - There have been alarming changes in the weather due to global warming with so many snowcapped mountains melting.

CHAPTER 3

SUMMARY WRITING

This chapter is dedicated to learning and understanding the dynamics of writing a crisp yet inclusive summary highlighting all the common points.

Summary writing

Most of us have been writing summaries from primary school itself. Summary means a clear, concise version of the main idea or crux of the passage or writeup. To be precise, one has to not extensively write everything described in the passage but choose the main themes and topics.

The summary question is as a part of continuous writing exercise in the exam and mostly focusses on a part of the passage. Therefore, writing an IGCSE summary is a different ball game from writing a generic summary.

Some of the salient points of a summary in this format are:

1. Stick to the word limit of 120 words for IGCSE (0500) and IGCSE (9-1/0990).
2. Read the question like a hawk spots its prey, that is, be exactly sure of what is asked and just focus on that.
3. Don't skip the main idea or the themes.
4. Learn the art of making your piece compact by combining multiple sentences into complex sentences as well as omitting repeated thoughts and words.
5. Summary in IGCSE is minimalistic and one has to write what is extremely important and focussed in the extract.
6. The language need not be very flowery like descriptive writing but use of certain **refined** words, **especially connectors, adverbs, verbs and some adjectives are ideal.**
   For example, if there is a solution that is suggested but which is not very ideal, employ the connectors like However, Despite, Inspite of etc.

7. There is no need of an elaborate introduction. For e.g. if the question is, 'What are the reasons the main character, John, chose to participate in an Iron man event?' the summary should commence with the statement, 'The multiple reasons of John to participate in an Iron man event were firstly the ….

8. For a specific summary, conclusion might not be required but for the whole passage summary, the conclusion should be short yet defining the end properly.

Please note, summarising in IGCSE requires sharp thinking and writing skills to include only what is required and adhering to the word limit and at the same time not leaving key data.

Solved Example- 1

Question - According to the text, what are the worries and concerns some people have about the new meal-replacement products now available? You must use continuous writing (not note form) and use your own words as far as possible. Your summary should not be more than 120 words.

Up to 10 marks are available for the content of your answer and up to 5 marks for the quality of your writing.

Tips:

1. The question strongly mentions continuous writing and no note form. Hence, don't use bullet points.
2. Word limit -120 words. Please don't write under the word limit. About 10% over the word limit is acceptable. However, don't over exceed the word limit too.
3. It is a 15 marks question, hence annotate atleast 10-15 points.
4. Read the question very carefully. The summary needs to be only about the worries and concerns that people have about the new products. Hence, don't get distracted and mention everything.
5. Content – It forms the major bulk of writing. Hence, mention all the concerns and worries in your own words using right verbs, adverbs and adjectives. Use connectives (subordinating conjunctions) such as 'So, Therefore, However, Yet, Despite' etc. to convey the opinions.

6. Last but not the least, in the main text annotate / mark the worries and concern that the people have about the new products so that it will be easier to form a logical essay.

Text- A complete diet in a time-saving way? (Source of Question-CIE Paper May/June 2017)

The writer discusses some of the meal-replacement products such as protein shakes, gels and powders that are currently available. You can divide the world into two groups of people: those who drink protein shakes for breakfast and those who don't. I am firmly in the latter. It's fair to say that I'm not the target market for the lucrative line of trendy meal-replacement products all tapping into the idea that food is old-fashioned, inconvenient and boring. Apparently, there's now a more hi-tech, whizz-bang way of delivering the same nutrients more efficiently in the form of gels and powders.

Yum. I'm almost tempted to try the 'bespoke vitamin and mineral blend' described as 'an all-natural, vegan formula' – until I talk to Joanna Blythman, an investigative food writer. She scoffs at the idea. 'These products contain technologically altered hi-tech ingredients. You're talking about industrial food chemistry where basic ingredients are being mucked around with and transformed. There are these very intense chemical sweeteners in there. There's sucralose; that's something like 200 times sweeter than sugar. There's maltodextrin – that's another sweetener. And xylitol – that's another one. It's all just rubbish. Then there's 'pea protein', which sounds good, doesn't it, but what is it? Peas treated with a number of complex, chemical reactions to extract some sort of beige powder.' It does raise the question of why you'd want to eat that. On Twitter, I find a Swiss software developer who tells me he's been eating nothing else for weeks. 'I've just moved to the city

Comment [JL1]: 1. Modified ingredients - A concern

Commented [JL2]: 2. Basic ingredients are messed with

Commented [JL3]: 3. Very intense sweetness, hazardous for heath

Commented [JL4]: 4. Lot of other harmful sweeteners

Commented [JL5]: 5. Artificially prepared pea protein - why would you eat it?

and it's an effort to find time to cook each evening. I have a very healthy lifestyle and like eating healthily. I read about it and thought I'd give it a go.' My running partner, Catherine, is exactly the type of person who drinks protein shakes for breakfast. At the end of our run, she pulls out her 'lunch' from her rucksack. 'It's OK,' she says. I'm not sure. We may want to maximise the health benefits of food, but the research simply isn't there yet, and what about the emotional, cultural and social well-being aspects of food? We're not robots: food is more than just fuel. Appetite is such a fundamental drive. Food is part of what we do every day to make our lives a bit nicer. If you've had a bad day, it's just that little nice thing you can do for yourself. And these products just don't get that at all.

> Commented [JL6]: 6. What about the emotional, cultural and social well being associated with food.
>
> Commented [JL7]: 7. Food is so much more than just energy
>
> Commented [JL8]: 8. It is a natural urge
>
> Commented [JL9]: 9. These products can't elevate your mood or make lives bit nicer.

Sample Summary:

*Some of the key concerns and alarming worries that people are having about these new meal replacement products are the way these products are manufactured altering their chemical ingredients in a high-tech and potentially **detrimental** manner. Products such as multivitamins may initially sound appealing but contain a battery of harmful chemicals such as sweetners (sucralose), xylitol and synthetic proteins. **Another concern** is about food such as protein shakes being **excessively** marketed as health friendly though food is just not about calories and weight but has a deeper connection to basic desires, mental, social and cultural wellbeing which these artificial products cannot cater to. Worries are expressed to replace wholesome meals with these products that can have lot of deleterious impacts on mental health and the fundamental drive to enjoy food.*

> Commented [D10]: Coming directly on the point without an elaborate introduction
>
> Commented [D11]: Use of powerful vocabulary
>
> Commented [D12]: Use of connectives
>
> Commented [D13]: Appropriate adverbs

Solved Example - 2:
Text B: Tough Mudder (Source: CIE June 2022)

Jayden Dee is a participant in Tough Mudder, an obstacle course endurance race. In this article, he has been interviewed by his local newspaper, the Redmond Gazette (RG).

Jayden Dee knows about hard work and dedication, as the 27-year-old athlete and army captain is keen to prove. Despite missing the deadline to enter this year's Tough Mudder World Championship, airing on national television this weekend, he repeatedly emailed the company responsible for the event, asking to be included in the endurance contest. Eventually, they gave in and allowed Dee to compete.

Tough Mudder isn't his first competition. Dee, who spent four years at a prestigious military school on a wrestling scholarship, competed in his first Ironman triathlon a few months ago. But the Tough Mudder event is something different altogether. It's billed as 'the most insane race around', featuring obstacles with names such as 'Kong' and 'Devil's Beard'. Participants bench-press sandbags, climb walls, crawl and run through mud, among other things that will make them wet, tired and dirty.

Tough Mudder was held earlier this summer, with entrants competing for a substantial cash prize. We spoke to Dee beforehand about his preparation.

RG: How did you find out about Tough Mudder?

Dee: I found out online through social media, and I was like, 'I think I can compete with these guys'. I literally stayed up all night watching the one-hour special from last year's competition, and that's when I was hooked. I said to myself, 'I need to find a way to get into this.'

RG: Is that typical of you?

Dee: Well I was super-competitive through school, and then I kinda needed a break, which was good because I went to Hawaii. So the last four years in Hawaii, I stayed active, but also made a point to relax. I always knew I'd come back and compete in something. I just was waiting for the right time. Then I did the Ironman competition and got the bug again. I was in really good shape when I found out about this event. It seemed like now was the time to come back.

RG: How do you see yourself doing?

Dee: I want to win the whole thing! A lot of my role models, people I really look up to are in this competition, so I'm extremely realistic, but I also truly believe I can win. So I'm gonna do my best.

I want to represent Redmond well. It's easy for people to forget where they come from, but I don't. This way while I'm home on leave I can get a chance to inspire kids as the 'Redmond Guy'.

According to Text B, why did Jayden Dee want to take part in this particular event?

You must use continuous writing (not note form) and use your own words as far as possible.

Your summary should not be more than 120 words. Up to 10 marks are available for the content of your answer and up to 5 marks for the quality of your writing.

After annotating the points pertaining to the reasons of participation of Jayden Dee in the Tough Mudder event, it can be summarised as follows:

There are multiple reasons for Jayden Dee to participate in the Tough Mudder competition. Primarily, being a previous Ironman competitor, he is more than eager to try his hand at this extreme endurance event because he feels he has it in him to be a winner too.

He is also extremely fond of the sport and is quite glued to watching these events. Secondly, most of his idols are participating and therefore he is also highly motivated to give it a go. After a rejuvenating vacation in Hawaii, he is physically and mentally ready to compete along with the fact that he really wants to be a role model for the kids of his Redmond community since he really feels, he is a hardcore Redmond guy.

CHAPTER 4

LETTER WRITING

The type of letters normally asked in the examination are either formal letters or informal ones.

One of the unique aspects of letter writing in the IGCSE format is that they are based on related information in the inserts and are therefore included under directed writing. Therefore, the key factors to be kept in mind are:

1. Read the text in the insert properly and precisely retain the summary in your mind.
2. Despite the fact that the letter is based upon the material in the texts, **strictly write the letter in your own words.**
3. Pay special attention to **the bullet points** that are asked in the question.
4. **Don't exceed the word limit** or write excessively **below the word limit.**
   Writing concisely yet comprehensively is the key and that comes with lot of writing practice.
5. **For a letter, the word limit is about 250 -350 words.**
6. A letter, whether formal or informal, can be properly spaced in **five medium sized paragraphs.**

Tips:

1. One must take advantage of this task since it is easier than some of the other writing types such as an article, speech, interview etc.
2. The format is quite familiar since it is taught from primary school itself and therefore, if the letter is to the point with sophisticated language, vocabulary and answering all the questions, it can help you to notch up your scores in Directed writing.

Formal letters

As the word suggests, formal letters are addressed to officials, professionals or people that might not be your acquaintances as well as the reasons or contexts that you are addressing might not be personal.

Structure of Formal letters:

1. The letter should start with a greeting or salutation. Earlier, most of the time, 'Respected Sir/Madam' was treated as a gold standard but now, even 'Dear Sir/Madam' is allowed and accepted well.

2. The address is written in top left corner such as 'To, XYZ (Name), Address: Ford Street'... etc. It is not compulsory to write address.

3. Date and subject of the letter can be mentioned. Date can be written at the top right corner.

4. The end of a letter is marked by expressing gratitude or thanks.

   For different target individuals, different phrases can be used.

   For e.g., For someone you know personally as a work colleague or boss,

   you could use, 'Yours faithfully'/ 'Yours truly'.

   For someone whom you don't know well or addressing for the first time,

   you could use, 'Yours sincerely'.

5. For a formal letter, it is of utmost importance that one sticks to the subject and mentions it in the first or at the most beginning of the second paragraph.

6. The body paragraphs can be one or two and of a good or sizeable length.

7. The language needs to be formal and sophisticated.

For example, while commencing a letter addressed to the city mayor about lack of sanitation in your area, it can be written as:

I would earnestly like to bring to your notice certain alarming concerns about sanitation in our area.

8. A certain amount of precision and well-rounded arguments are expected.

For example, in the above mentioned letter prompt about sanitation, some of the key arguments can be:

It has been consistently observed that the trash is not collected on a daily basis because of which the number of mosquitoes and rodents has significantly

increased. It is a serious health concern especially due to the fact that 3-4 residents in the area are already suffering from deadly diseases like dengue.

There is a continuous effluvium or malodour that is present in the vicinity and we really feel embarrassed to call our friends and relatives due to this issue.

9. The letter conclusion is extremely critical and needs to include the gist of the main subject followed by gratitude based phrases and ending.

For e.g. Awaiting your prospective reply / Hopeful for a favourable consideration/ I would really appreciate if you could assist me in this matter etc.

Solved Example:

Write a letter to the mayor of your city highlighting the persistent lack of sanitation and growing hazards about the same.

To,_____Date:

The Mayor,

XYZ City Council,

UK.

Sub: Concerns about local sanitation.

Respected Sir/Dear Sir,

I, would hereby, earnestly like to bring it to your notice that I live in the vicinity of Ford drive and there has been a serious concern about sanitation and hygiene in the neighbourhood.

For the past three months, the garbage is not picked up duly on a daily basis as a result of which, there is lot of organic and inorganic waste lying at the sides that is potentially deleterious for health of the local residents. There have been 3-4 cases of Dengue detected in the last month mostly due to the increasing number of mosquitoes because of the stale waste.

There is also a likelihood of more rodents and infections because of the same. There is so much of malodor because of the same that most of us are embarrassed to pass the street or call relatives or friends at our residences.

This is an alarming situation and more so can have a detrimental impact on children's health and safety too along with the adults.

For last three months, the issue is lingering and no measures have been adopted by the local authorities to dispose this waste or sanitise the surrounding area. As a community, our general health and well being is at risk and this serious problem needs to addressed on an urgent basis.

More awareness about the proper disposal of waste has to be created among the masses and residents must be encouraged to responsibly dispose waste too.

I, therefore, kindly appeal to you to please look into the matter at the earliest and take the necessary action.

Awaiting your further reply in this regard.

Thanking You,

Yours faithfully,

Anita.

Informal Letters

As the word suggests, informal letters are addressed to people that are your acquaintances as well as the reasons or contexts that are personal or related. In the IGCSE English course (0500) and IGCSE (9-1)0990 course, informal letters are majorly asked as a part of directed writing task either in Paper 1 or Paper 2.

Structure of Informal letters:

1. The letter should start with a greeting or salutation such as 'Dear' or 'My dear' daughter, son, friend etc. (Can Include names or just ABC/XYZ).
2. There is no need to write address for an informal letter.
3. Date can be written at the top right corner.
4. The end of a letter is marked by expressing gratitude or thanks with a range of phrases such as Yours lovingly, Your loving daughter/son/niece, Yours sincerely for accepting invitations, Yours truly, Kind regards etc.

5. For an informal letter, the introductory statement must be informal without directly jumping to the topic. Some of the introductory statements can be: Hope you are well/ I hope this letter finds you in the pink of health and spirits/ It has been a very long time since we met and hoping to see you soon etc.
6. The informal letter can be elaborate with 2-3 body paragraphs and of a good or sizeable length.
7. The language need not be curt and too formal. On the other hand, it can be little informal, conversational and warm.
8. Since it is a directed writing task, the bullet points mentioned in the question should be aptly highlighted and not ignored.

Sample Question

Read Text A and Text B and answer the following question: (Source: Cambridge IGCSE 0500 – June 2023 Insert 23)

A young child in your family has been selected to join an intensive training programme for their chosen sport and is eager to join. The child's parents have asked for your views about whether or not their child should join. Write a letter to the child's parents.

In your letter you should:

- *evaluate the views, attitudes and ideas given in both texts*
- *discuss the factors the parents should consider before deciding*
- *based on what you have read, give your views on whether or not the child and their family will benefit from the programme.*

Base your letter on what you have read in both texts, **but be careful to use your own words. Address both of the bullet points. Write about 250 to 350 words.**

Up to 15 marks are available for the content of your answer, and up to **25 marks for the quality of your writing.**

Let us spot key points in both Text A and Text B for comprehensively collating all the arguments for the letter.

Text A

This text is taken from an article in which the parents of young sportspeople describe their experiences.

Sofia Polowyj, the mother of twin nine-year-old aspiring gymnasts, says that gymnastics is in their blood. 'My husband and I met as young gymnasts, so we know about the joys and pitfalls of the sport, although then there was just the glory of medals to aim for. It's tough on them – the early mornings in the gym, the strict diets, the school holidays spent in training camp rather than at the seaside. But they rarely complain and we're with them every step of the way to make sure they enjoy their successes and refocus when they don't perform so well. [**Commented [D14]:** Sacrifices made to succeed but the glory of it is exciting enough]

Obviously, I want them to succeed and if they ultimately choose a different path, well, that's fine too.'

Budding footballer 10-year-old Ranit Myska, has already played in several international tournaments in Spain and Singapore, organised by his training academy in India. His father, a doctor, funds his training and his foreign travel, and believes that his son benefits hugely from such opportunities. 'I know some parents think I'm insane,' he says, 'and it costs a lot in my time and money but the relentless emphasis on academics when I was young wasn't healthy either.' [**Commented [D15]:** Inspite of the excessive costs in terms of time and money, it is totally worth it plus focussing on just academics is not very wholesome.]

Ranit's ambition is to join a major football team's programme when he's 15, so he's dedicated and committed to his rigorous training, but he's also doing well in school. 'The determination he's developing in his football has spilled over into his academic work,' says his father. 'There's no downside for him, despite the arduous training and the sacrifices we make as a family.' [**Commented [D16]:** Indulging in sports boosts academic performance too]

In the UK, Sarah Sage's experience with her young athlete daughter has been mixed, but she has few regrets. Her daughter was singled out at school by her sports teacher for what was described as 'her prodigious natural talent' and the next four years were a blur of training and competition. 'Niggling injuries didn't deter her, and she loved her athletics family at the academy. Eventually though, she began to see her school friends' lives as more varied, less intense. She struggled with having every minute of her day pre-planned with no time left for spontaneity or just hanging out.

There were tears when she gave up her dream of elite athletics, but she still enjoys running. A punishing training regime at a young age doesn't suit everyone, however talented they are.'

Text B- Should we rethink elite sports for kids?

Given the enormous incomes elite sportspeople can earn, it's no wonder that in many countries across the globe, programmes that aim to identify and develop future elite athletes have been established.

Once selected, potential elite footballers, cyclists, gymnasts and others can spend many years being moulded and trained to fulfil their ambitions. These programmes, once entered, can shape the lives of children, and those of their families, for a long time.

It's thought by some coaches that specialising in a specific sport early in childhood is essential to achieve elite levels of success. Just like ballet dancers and musicians, it pays to start early. In sports such as gymnastics and diving, athletes usually peak in their late teens, so specialising in childhood is considered crucial. Athletic careers are also inevitably shorter than most other career choices and children, parents and trainers are often aware of that. Many children who specialise early develop personal qualities of resilience and dedication that would shame an adult.

However, some psychologists suggest that if a child doesn't have other hobbies or doesn't try new activities, it can make them feel like their identity is solely tied to the sport they specialise in, which can affect their development detrimentally.

> Commented [D24]: Downsides of indulging intensively in a single sports activity

Delaying intense specialisation might give a young athlete more time to develop outside of their sport. Some think that if young athletes can try a range of different sports, perhaps eventual success at elite levels is more likely, not less. However, with safeguards in place, many child athletes grow up to look back on their years of intense training with pride and gratitude, even if they never make the grade in the elite world.

> Commented [D25]: Other side of the coin – Not just focusing on intense expertise

> Commented [D26]: Overarching benefits

Once the relevant points have been identified, they have to be coherently paraphrased as follows:

Sample Answer

Dear Suresh, 26/09/2023

I hope this letter finds you all in the best of spirits. I am fine here too. Recently, when you called me regarding the decision of sending Yug for professional football, I did think about the whole scenario very seriously and would like to share my views and suggestions that I could gather in the last few days.

> Commented [D27]: Informal beginning. Don't jump on the topic straightaway.

There is so much of literature which suggests that playing any kind of sports is highly beneficial for children as it has far reaching benefits than just pleasure or recreation. There have been so many experiences of children playing elite or competitive sport cited by their parents as being highly transformative and value added for not just the children but also themselves.

> Commented [D28]: Reference to the content in the text A in terms of benefits

The intense training, both in terms of physical and mental fitness and the various sacrifices that the parents and children have to make in the process is very rewarding .A child' character, discipline, go- getter attitude and endurance is developed because of the same and such attributes are sometimes not even present in adults. This becomes a matter of pride for both the parents and their offspring.

I, therefore, strongly think that you must enroll Yug for the sport that he fancies or is passionate about. Firstly, football is an elite sport and it can be, therefore, very lucrative and life changing.

Considering all the benefits of indulging in sports, I think that Yug will be shaped very properly and will gain the key skills required to face life and competition.

Although, sometimes, he might feel he is losing on normal life compared to other kids or he may completely feel lost without the sport. These reactions are normal and do not outweigh the multiple merits of choosing sport.

Holistically, I strongly recommend you to think deeply about this matter and do not make any further delay in enrolling him for football since the experts always assert that it is best to start early so that actual expertise can be gained by teenage years.

I hope I have answered some of your questions and if you need any further assistance you know that I am just a call away.

Rest all is fine. Please give my sincere regards to everyone in the family.

Awaiting your reply.
Take care.
Regards,

Anil

CHAPTER 5
DIARY ENTRY AND JOURNAL WRITING

Diary Writing

Diary writing is a form of recount or expressing your thoughts, feelings, experiences and happenings. Diary is a personalised piece of writing since it shows what has happened to you.

For example, you might be asked to write a diary entry about the most memorable experience at school or how you felt when your best friend was leaving the country for good or about your experience on the day of field trip organised by your school etc.

Most important considerations while attempting a diary entry are enlisted as follows:

1. First and foremost, it is of utmost importance to use first person to write a diary entry because it describes about the events or things happened to you or your thoughts and feelings about them.

    E.g. - I was utterly shocked by my best friend's behaviour. Here, 'I', the first person brings more relatability and relevance to the write-up.

2. Since diary writing is mostly done to describe about some event, experience or thought about the recent past or more distant experience, use of past tense is appropriate.

3. Vividly describing your thoughts, sentiments, experiences and observations is the key and should be included in each paragraph. Topic sentences are important.

    E.g. – As we landed in Kashmir, I was flabbergasted to see the beautiful tea gardens, the ever-flowing cool breeze, absolutely crisp air and all I savoured was organic tea.

4. Use of powerful adjectives, verbs, sensory words and imagery can actually create the picture of the scene in the minds of the reader.

5. The usual structure of paragraphs can be used making sure new idea or event is mentioned in every new paragraph for better flow.

6. Diaries or recounts are written in a chronological or sequential order of the events. Hence, it is vital to use conjunctions such as initially, primarily, firstly, next, then, followed by, consequently, etc. to indicate when they happened or their context or what happened before or after or cause and effect.

7. Detailed explanation to add minute details is significant to give the audience the exact idea of the actions, consequences and experiences. E.g. – That night was as horrifying as walking alone in a forbidden forest with wolves and bears waiting to ambush.

8. It is highly important to use emotive language so that the reader can exactly connect with your thoughts, sentiments and viewpoint. Use emotive language so the reader understands your point of view.
E.g. - I was shattered. I had put my blood, sweat and tears into the preparation. But, I failed to succeed.

9. Varied sentence types- Use of shorter sentences or exclamatory sentences, repetition of words is important to convey the emotion of surprise, shock, disgust etc.

10. Varied punctuation- Use of exclamation marks, ellipsis, commas, colons, question marks, dashes can add richness to the write-up.

Sample Question

Passage A: Mikaela and Jane (0500, w18 qp 22)

In this passage, Mikaela waits for Jane who is shopping at the market.

Mikaela watched the world pass by the window. She nodded and smiled at each and every one of these liberated pedestrians, drawn into a current in the direction of the market. Their wheeled shopping bags bounced and

> **Commented [DJL34]:** Bullet point 1 What did Mikaela and Jane do in the morning?

bounded behind them in enthusiastic obedience. The road was a sea of movement, and no one looked up at the imprisoned figure in the window.

Mikaela sighed, allowing small breaths of warm air to escape and form cloudy shapes on the glass, into which she drew stick-people jumping, skipping and running. After a while, words replaced the sighs: 'I hope she won't take too long.' Her chest felt a little tight again and she screwed up her face. She knew she just had to be patient. She pressed the control under her right hand. It whirred a little, but nothing moved. *** Jane consulted her list: quite a lot of groceries this week, but she knew where she would find them.

> **Commented [DJL35]:** Specific points about Mikaela and her state of mind - Can be included in Bullet 1

She enjoyed shopping in the large market, the buzz, the colour, the unpredictability. She held her purse closely inside her pocket. You did have to be careful in these places. There were desperate people everywhere. She thought about Mikaela. Yes, she would be quick. No loitering around those soap stalls, where pink, amber and fiery red, pebble-shaped bars lured and distracted you with scents of unexpected and delicious promise.

Ahead, the market was beginning to wake up. Jane enjoyed watching it at this time of the day. It was like a large beast, groaning in dismay at being prodded into life, its elongated body undulating and rippling, as the stall-holders pinned and adjusted fluttering awnings and canvas covers to their correct positions. Metal trolleys squealed in angry protest as their wheels careered crazily over the tarmac to be eventually butted up against the stalls.

Here they disgorged their contents, their items of sale, slipping and sliding across shiny surfaces. Jane consulted her list again. She moved quickly through the sea of busy vendors, avoiding stacked boxes of cheerful nick-nacks and rails of colourful clothing, until she came to the back of the market. She avoided looking at the soap stall nearby, trying not to sniff its heavenly aromas, and waited patiently for Niki, the fruit and vegetable vendor. Niki was busy at his stall. Labels needed fastening to large crates of white cabbage and sweet potatoes.

> Commented [DJL36]: Jane's activities- Bullet 1

Jane quickly helped him to pile up stacks of melons and mangoes. 'Yesterday's stock on the counter, please, Jane. We have to sell that first. Today's underneath. There.' Niki pointed under a flapping red cover. 'How is Mikaela?' Niki now stood with his hands on his hips, surveying Jane. He smiled. He has

such a kind smile, Jane thought. He has always been a good friend. 'She is still weak. She has this cough. We hoped the doctor would come today, but it will be tomorrow now. One of the wheels on her chair jammed this morning. I can move it if I tilt the chair slightly onto its back wheels, but she can't move it herself.' Niki looked concerned. 'That's no good. It's too heavy for you. I will pop by tonight, and fix it. Here – let's see that list. Just the freshest ingredients for Mikaela.' He lifted the red cover and began to move boxes around.

> Commented [D37]: Relationship between Mikaela and Niki

Soon a heap of the freshest fruit and vegetables filled Jane's basket. 'Thank you, Niki.' Jane paid the vendor and began to walk quickly away. Niki watched the urgency with which she weaved her way through crowds. His eye fell on the small, brightly coloured piles of soap on the stall next door. She deserved a bit of a treat, too, he thought. *** Jane let herself into the house. 'Grandma, I will make the potato and onion soup now. Do you want to come and watch?' She grabbed the handles, carefully tilted the wheelchair backwards and slowly edged it into the small kitchen. Mikaela sighed happily. 'You are such a good girl. I was worried you might take a long time. I know a lot of those stalls are so tempting. After this, we can play cards and you can tell me about the market this morning. How is Niki?

> Commented [D38]: Bullet point no 2 What did Jane do when she returned home?

You are Mikaela from Passage A.

Write your diary entry for the day's events.

In your diary entry you should include your thoughts and feelings about:

- What you and Jane did during the morning
- What happened after Jane returned and later that evening
- Your relationship with Jane and Niki

Base your diary entry on what you have read in Passage A, but be careful to use your own words. Address each of the three bullet points.

Begin your diary entry, 'Dear Diary, Today has been quite eventful …' Write about 250 to 350 words. Up to 15 marks are available for the content of your answer, and up to 5 marks for the quality of your writing.

Sample Answer:

Dear Diary,

Today has been quite eventful especially because Jane had gone for errands to the nearest market. [Commented [D39]: Description about Bullet point 1 : What did Jane and Mikaela do A diary entry should always describe the emotions, feelings and experiences in detail]

Despite being stranded at home on a wheel chair, I jumped on the opportunity to watch the hustle bustle outside the window. People had amassed in huge numbers for grocery shopping.

The shrieking of their shopping bags, their running helter skelter added lot of zeal in me. I literally sensed viewing the whole world from my window pane. Amidst this boom of activity, seeing people running, rushing, I felt a sense of weariness and tried to breathe as much as I could. After a while though, I started feeling restless and a little anxious. I was eagerly waiting for Jane and felt a little heavy in my chest. [Commented [D40]: Bullet 3- Mikaela's emotional dependence on Niki (Nature of relationship with Niki)]

To make matters worse, my wheel chair got a bit stuck and I again felt a thump in my heart. On the other hand, Jane had a long list of groceries but she was resolute to find each of items and I trusted her. Jane thoroughly enjoyed shopping amidst the shopping buzz, the vibrancy of vegetables and fruits and the extreme crowd. I knew that she would not waste much time window shopping because she was always concerned about me and the fact that I am alone at home.

After shopping, she waited calmly for Niki, her friend and the fruit and the vegetable vendor. She helped him with the vendoring duties.

When Jane returned home, she quickly made potato and onion soup for me and carefully held my wheel chair and brought me in the kitchen to accompany her. We had a nice chat and decided to play cards. She also told me about her friend Niki, who is a very gentle lad. He enquired about my health and Jane informed him about my cough and the jammed wheel chair.

Niki, instantly agreed to come in the evening and help us with fixing the chair. He was Mikaela's good buddy after all. Niki, like Jane, was very much concerned about me and that was indeed heartening!

Journal entry

Unlike diary entry, which is a personal retelling of your state of mind, emotions, dreams etc., a journal entry is a recount of your work/study day, experiences, feelings and observations. Writers use it extensively to vent their sentiments and experiences or to kick start their creativity.

Both these writing forms are written in first person (I, my, myself, mine etc).

The language should be very conversational describing what exactly you felt, saw or desired. The tone is neither too formal nor too flowery- it is real and authentic. Use of key adjectives, verbs, connectors, exclamations, rhetorical questions is desirable.

Rest all the rules are similar to those of diary writing such as appealing to the emotions of the reader, varying sentence structure, expressing the emotions in detail and literally talking to the reader.

Regarding the format of journal entry, kindly insert date and time on the left hand corner. It is not essential to start with a greeting like Dear diary.

For journal writing, the observations during the day and the impact they had on you is critical. The tone of your writing should be self-reflective.

The tense should be past or future tense, depending on whether one is writing about recent past or anticipating future events.

Sample Question (0500 –May/June 2019 –QP 22)

Imagine you are the zookeeper.

Later that day you write in your journal reflecting on your feelings about life now and how things have changed.

Write your journal. In your journal, you should:

- describe what you do each day, why you do it and how that makes you feel
- explain what you have noticed about the boy and his father and your feelings about each of them.
- consider how things have changed for you and the world around you since you first started working at the zoo and suggest what you think the future may hold for you.

Base your journal on what you have read in Passage A, but be careful to use your own words. Address each of the three bullet points. Begin your journal, "Today was..."

Write about 250 to 350 words.

Up to 15 marks are available for the content of your answer, and up to 5 marks for the quality of your writing.

Sample insert -0500-May June 2019 Insert 22

Passage A: The last zookeeper

This story is set more than one hundred years in the future. It describes a boy and his father on one of their regular visits to a zoo.

The father remembers visiting the zoo 50 years earlier when he was a boy and the zoo was busier. The zookeeper has worked there since the day the zoo first opened. The boy stared at the zookeeper hobbling along.

> **Commented [D45]:** Bullet 1

Occasionally, this aged man would stumble, emit a pained grunt, then continue. The dented metal feed-bucket in his fist swung ponderously, banging against his knee. The bones in his hand, the gnarled knuckles, ropy tendons and veins stood out from the effort of carrying the heavy weight. The tissue-thin skin, mottled with age, was inhabited by ghosts of forgotten injuries, secret stories of wounds the boy would never know.

> **Commented [D46]:** Bullet 3 – How the work has taken toll on the zookeepr

The boy wondered what it would feel like to hold that hand, to touch the baggy covering and feel it slide over the brittle bones beneath the fingers, the time-withered muscle. His eyes slipped to his own hand, a smaller replica of his father's – both puffy with flesh, skin devoid of blemishes. Beneath their perfected surfaces, bright red serum circulated, delivering rich nourishment with exquisite precision and dependability.

> **Commented [D47]:** Bullet 2- observations about the child and father

Unlike the old man's, their palms were dry, cool despite the humidity of the day. The zookeeper paused outside the cage and jangled his key ring, repeating the movement until the wisp of a shape, a lighter shadow, suggested the presence of some hulking wild beast inside.

> **Commented [D48]:** Bullet 2- observations about the child and father

Glass grey eyes glistened, briefly catching sunlight and seeming to peer out almost intelligently. The key turned in the lock.

The old man tugged the door open. The boy had witnessed the same wordless dialogue every day for the past three years; he knew it all by

> **Commented [D49]:** Bullet 1- Kind of work the zookeeper did

heart. The animal still did not emerge. It never did at this point. The acrid tang of the lab-grown meat in the bucket stung the boy's nose: the flesh had begun to spoil immediately after it was removed from its sterile bath. The zookeeper extracted a pale slab of 'meat'. It hit the cement outside the cage with an unquestionably organic sound, attracting frenzied swarms of flies. The boy could see and hear them buzzing, hovering. Even technological advances of recent decades had not succeeded in eradicating these pests.

Minds, augmented by artificial intelligence, could still not calculate a solution to this problem. 'Some species follow no mathematical formula,' his father commented. Most did, the boy was told. Humans, for example, were very mathematical in their behaviour. There were exceptions – occasionally individuals still defied being reduced to basic principles and programs.

The old man extracted a filthy handkerchief from his overalls and dabbed his forehead. Even as he did so, new beads of sweat erupted. 'Jumbe?' The man's frail voice trembled and cracked. He waited. 'Jumbe, come out and eat.' The boy could almost feel the keeper hoping ... but the shape behind the cage door still didn't move. At last the old man sighed. His shoulders fell. His back stooped more. He reached over and swiped at the metal plate beside the gate.

There was a soft whirr, almost too quiet to hear. Finally, with a tired groan, the animal shuffled out. The boy came daily to witness this feeding. Somehow, he always expected the outcome to be different. 'Why does he bother?' he asked his father every visit. 'Why?' Turn over 'Old habits are hard to break,' his father

told him again. The boy felt something like disappointment, but accepted the usual answer. He supposed understanding would come, once final electrical connections had been made and his father had fully imparted knowledge into him. The ancient beast's pelt, bleached bone-white by unrelenting sun, was badly tattered. Bare spots betrayed where fur rubbed painfully against metal. The animal turned, exposing old tears in its side. ==Through these raggedly sutured gaps, the boy could see underlying musculature, atrophied meat and churning gears. He wondered how many times the zookeeper had repaired the damage. 'I don't know,' the father answered automatically.==

'That information isn't available.' The boy was tempted to question the old man, but the father gave the boy's hand a warning squeeze. The boy read again the faded plaque displayed outside the cage:

> Commented [D50]: Bullet 3 – what has changed

African Lion Extinct. This male, the last known individual of its kind, died of wasting disease in 2039. It was reanimated at the Institute for the Preservation of Wholly-biological Artefacts and added to the zoo's collection. It is the only remaining fully functioning cybernetised African lion on public display.

His father moved. 'Come on – the monkey's next.' The boy didn't care about the monkey whose cage was before the only empty one, near the zoo's exit. This zookeeper captivated him.

In the whole entire menagerie, this ancient man's dedication to a world long-since dead remained an unsolved equation in the boy's siliconised brain.

> Commented [D51]: Bullet 2- observations about the child and father

Steps:

Firstly, annotate the relevant points according to the bullet points targeted in the question.

Bullet 1-describe what you do each day, why you do it and how that makes you feel

Bullet 2-explain what you have noticed about the boy and his father and your feelings about each of them.

Bullet 3 - consider how things have changed for you and the world around you since you first started working at the zoo and suggest what you think the future may hold for you.

Sample Answer:

Today was yet another day where I reached the zoo early morning literally panting for breath.

For the last so many days, I feel so exhausted and completely enervated and the toll that this work has taken on my body is not clearly visible in my atrophied body, conspicuous veins, trembling limbs and extreme paleness.

When I started this unique job about 50 years ago, I was completely excited and looking forward to each day.

Things have totally changed for the worst wherein I am simply stretching day after day because I can't run away from my duties.

The animals, even if they are cybernetised wait for me since there are very few souls who really care for them. As I was walking, feeling highly wearied,

I came across this familiar face, a doting father with his curious son waiting to explore the marvel of the new age zoo.

I distinctly remember this gentleman, who used to visit my zoo regularly as a child and now his child had taken a new leaf. I was quite enervated to be honest but had a little sprint in the stride to see the boy accompanying me so dearly and curiously to unfold of wilderness.

I was given this mammoth task to look after lot of cages and we reached the vital one, that of the extinct African lion. Almost trembling, I tried to call him couple of times and finally barged into the cage. Off came the monster, almost replicated like the real one with lot of scars, lacerations, hurt and fatigue.

Surprisingly, the boy seemed a little disappointed with this digitally operated lion and was infact more curious and fascinated about my life as a zoo keeper.

Honestly, I am in two minds as to what will happen in future and for how long will I really have the nerve to continue this extremely laborious and monotonous job. I enjoyed the real animals but now I am left with the automated ones. How long will I persist, God knows.

CHAPTER 6

SPEECH WRITING

*S*peeches are very commonly asked in IGCSE Paper 1 as well as Paper 2 directed writing. Although they sound common and a little easier, crafting an excellent speech script requires lot of careful thinking, the right punches and the desired effect to convey the intended message perfectly.

As a type of persuasive piece, all the essentials need to be woven very meticulously with a solid introduction, engaging body paragraphs and a formidable conclusion.

Introduction or Opening -

Speeches are used for variable contexts: academic, professional, social, political etc. However, for any kind of context, the opening of speech needs to be extremely impactful and memorable. It is like getting audience's attention fixated on your subject matter.

Some of the tools used for writing an engaging introduction are:

1. Starting with a sense of alarm or a dramatic introduction. Especially useful for giving speeches on social, environmental or political issues. For e.g. For a speech on global warming, one can being with,
   Our Mother Earth has been weeping for ages. Have we not realised the irreversible harm that we have thrown upon her?
2. As used above, rhetorical questions are another vital instruments to start a speech and compel the reader to think and resonate with the matter.

Middle Body paragraphs-

The middle body paragraphs can be three. Each bullet point can be focussed in three body paragraphs. Focus on reinforcing the main points.

Conclusion:

The concluding paragraph of a speech is critical and if it is not powerful enough, the message may not effectively reach or engage the audience. Use of several phrases such as, "Thank you all for your patient ear" or "It was an absolute pleasure to get a chance to voice out on today's topic" or "Really hoping for a prospective future" are very fruitful.

Tools to enhance a speech:

1. Rule of three or tricolon: Three words or phrases describing the same point to add emphasis. For e.g. The leader was upbeat, unapologetic and vocal.
2. Hyperbole or Exaggeration: Using hyperbole or overstatements prudently is a key element of a truly impactful speech. E.g. Exaggerated rhetorical questions like, 'Is the mother earth not the victim of continual human abuse?'
3. Emotive language: Using personal pronouns such as 'we', 'our' etc. and using words and phrases that are emotionally moving.
4. Use of proverbs or expert quotes: It is quite a common practice to quote proverbs or sometimes some expert saying to add lot of appeal and impact to the speech.
5. Rhetorical questions as stated earlier can create that alarming effect.
6. Repetition: Repeating words or ideas has a special place in a speech. It can be used to add more emphasis.
7. Statistics /Data: Including key data, numbers or statistics adds lot of authenticity and rigour to a speech.
8. Use of cogent vocabulary.
9. An assertive and very persuasive tone.
10. Use of powerful adjectives, adverbs, exclamatory sentences, verbs and nouns.

Sample Task:

Imagine you are Andrei. You have noticed the changes in Lois which have made you reconsider how your business operates and decide to make some improvements. A few weeks later, you give a speech to other business owners.

In your speech you should explain:

- the nature of your business, what you hope to achieve and how successful it has been so far
- the concerns you have had about your staff
- the improvements you have made at GD as a result of speaking with Lois. Write the words of the speech.

Base your speech on what you have read in Text C, but be careful to use your own words. Address each of the three bullet points.

Begin your speech, 'My company, General Dexterity ...' Write about 250 to 350 words.

Following is the annotation of key points for the speech.

Text C: The Clement Street Soup and Sourdough Restaurant

Lois has moved away from the place where she grew up to work for a company called General Dexterity (GD) founded by a young businessman called Andrei. The company designs industry-leading robot arms for factories and needs talented computer-programmers to find ways to improve what their robots can do.

Commented [D52]: Background of Andrei and what the company does.

Day one, Andrei gave a guided tour of the company's underground base – a cavernous construction, formerly a car park. Towering rows of robot arms sweeping, grasping and lifting lined the cement floor. Their plastic cladding was coloured sky-blue, their contours friendly and capable with just the faintest suggestion of biceps – gentle swells sporting GD's logo, a lightning bolt. These were repetitive gestures, Andrei explained, currently executed by human muscles and minds. Repetition stifled human creativity, he said. Repetition belonged to robots.

Commented [D53]: Concerns of Andrei about the staff since work is very repetitive

I learned about the software I'd be working on and saw the founder's original prototype robot arm, a three-jointed limb taller than me. You could call, 'Arm, change task. Say hello!' and it would wave a wide, eager greeting – unlike my new workmates. Orientation week ended on Friday night. Then my job began. Not the following Monday. The next morning. Saturday. I had the feeling of being sucked – flop – into a pneumatic tube. Programmers at GD were almost exclusively young, distant, cold-eyed wraiths, in identical denim. They started early morning, working past midnight, in a hurry to be done, and rich. Each week the section manager, Peter, reminded us: We're on a mission to replace human labour – work harder. Programmers often slept at the office. Some nights I'd lie there, staring blankly at the ceiling and the braids of fibre ferrying data around the office. My parents were far away, locked in the frame of a video-chat window. I had no friends nearby. There was a knot in my stomach that wouldn't loosen. I existed in a state of stupor, brain flaccid, cells gasping. I couldn't get my turbine spinning. It was Peter who'd recommended switching to the meal-replacement, Slurry. 'It's what we all eat,' he said. At meal times, I sat in a corner of the empty cafeteria and slurped the grey gel. It would have been Slurry for 'dinner' as always, if I hadn't discovered, stuck to my apartment's door, a handwritten menu advertising a local delivery service. I'd just arrived home from work. My face felt brittle from stress – this wasn't unusual. I was already flagging after a single summer at my new job. I was supposed to be one of the bright new additions, the fresh-faced ones. My face wasn't fresh. My hair had gone flat and thin. My stomach hurt.

I wouldn't normally have been interested, but this menu, written in a dark confident script, intrigued me. At the top, in exuberant letters, was the restaurant's name and telephone number. The menu was compact: Spicy Soup, a Spicy Sandwich or a Combo (double spicy), all of which, the menu explained in its curling connectors, were vegetarian. The menu charmed me – as a result, my night, and my life, bent off on a different track. I called the number. A friendly voice answered, 'Hello! What can I make for you?' I ordered the Combo. Sometime later, my order arrived, delivered by a cheery young man with a heavy, hard-to-place accent: 'Good evening, my friend!' I dug in my pocket for cash, then thought to ask, 'What kind of food is this?' His face beamed. 'Real food, traditionally made. If you like it, I'll give you the recipe.' Sitting on my kitchen countertop – utterly bare in those days, free from any sign of food preparation – I consumed the first Combo (double spicy) of my life. The healing powers, physical and psychic, of the spicy soup made traditional noodle soup seem like dishwater. It was an elixir. The sandwich was spicier still, thin-sliced vegetables slathered with a fluorescent red sauce, the burn buffered by thick slabs of bread artfully toasted. First my stomach unclenched, then my brain. I let loose a long sigh that transformed into a rippling burp. I laughed out loud. That night, instead of fitfully reviewing the day's errors, I fell asleep soothed by spicy broth and dreams of baking that fragrant, fluffy sourdough bread.

Commented [D60]: The employees would have felt better if they had better food choices in the company

Some of the key points in the text:

1. A robotic arm manufacturing company founded by a young owner Andrei.
2. Their mission was to design arms for factories, replace human labour and work really hard.
3. They needed talented programmers who could adapt.
4. The work culture was too demanding and intense: working round the clock without any sleep or sleeping on the factory floor.
5. The whole pressure was taking a toll on Loi, the employee's physical and mental health.
6. She felt isolated, alone, depressed and extremely sick.

7. The food at the company was disgusting being a sticky gel –least palatable.
8. She was too stressed, had lost the glow on her face, despite being a young newbee and was feeling too helpless.
9. She tried delicious food from a new restaurant and felt relieved and a little rejuvenated. She sensed a need of a better catering facility at the factory.
10. The founder needed to provide better food, resting facilities and overall support at the workplace.

Sample Answer:

Dear all,

My company, General Dexterity, a leading manufacturer of robot arms for various industries has been on a mission to deliver state-of-the art robotic arm design, reduce human intervention and replace it with the automatons. [Commented [JL61]: Relevant introduction, use of interesting vocabulary]

On one hand, where we are so successful in achieving the corporate aims and objectives, on the other hand, it has taken an alarming toll on the overall state of the employees as well as the working environment. [Commented [JL62]: Putting forth the issue]

I can proudly say that we are definitely taking affirmative steps to deal with this.

The nature of the job entails a certain compromise on human creativity since most of the programmers are burning their midnight oil to come up with the best codes at the cost of their health, lack of sleep and severe toll on their mental well being. [Commented [JL63]: Nature of the job - Bullet 1]

Our mettlesome work culture has enabled us to produce industry topping robotic arms. However, when I spoke to one of the employees, I was appalled to see the serious ramifications of what we have dreamt to achieve.

I had never imagined that my employees would be forced to sleep on the mats or the corners in the company, mostly devoid of sleep, working round the clock with unhealthy or very meagre food creating the best quality product. What happens to their health and well being? It is going down the drains. [Commented [JL64]: Concerns about the staff -Bullet 2]

I mean as a chief of the organisation, I am taking necessary steps to seriously alleviate all this by providing a better working environment, food and resting facilities so that my employees are atleast happier doing what they do and that inturn keeps us satisfied and buoyant.

> **Commented [JL65]:** Steps taken by the boss

I hope you guys have a real learning out of all this and please don't repeat the mistakes that we committed and please take some time out of our busy schedules to communicate with the staff and support them as much as you can.

I am grateful for the patience you have shown in listening to me. Have a good day!

CHAPTER 7

INTERVIEW WRITING

*I*nterview writing is also one of the key directed writing types asked in both Paper 1 and Paper 2. As an interview is a conversation or discussion between two people, the writing style should be chatty, conversational and not excessively formal.

There are three bullet points posed as questions of the interview. It is ideally expected to find atleast 5 points per question in the text so that one can create a script worth 15 marks. 10 marks are attributed for quality of your writing which includes use of interesting vocabulary, varying sentence lengths, using exclamations or emotive connectors such as "well", "To start with" etc.

Use of shorter sentences such as 'I froze' / 'I was awestruck or spellbound 'also have a role. The answers prepared have to have the character's traits or characteristics as well as one should talk in detail about emotions, feelings and experiences and make them very appealing for the audience.

Use of personal pronouns is a must to make the experience relatable to the Interviewer and the wider target audience.

As far as punctuation is concerned use of colons after the words, Interviewer and Interviewee (Name) is required.

An exemplar is presented herewith:

Text C- The wild tigers of Ranthambore

The narrator, Val, is a photographer, author and documentary filmmaker. He has spent over 45 years living, working and campaigning at the tiger reserve in Ranthambore National Park, near the town of Sawai Madhopur (SM). In this extract from his book, Val remembers first travelling to the area by train from his city home as a young man in 1976.

Exiting the deserted station, I woke up the driver of a solitary horse-drawn carriage. In those days Sawai Madhopur (SM) boasted few motorised vehicles. The town wasn't prosperous. Numerous taxi-jeeps and buses taking chattering tourists into the park were still figments of shiny future ambition.

Garish hotel chains were yet to sprout, mushrooming along newly surfaced roads to the park. This was a sleepy town, sprawled untidily around the railway track, the only reason for its existence. Since then, local painters have decorated the station walls. Now murals of our tigers and other wildlife engage curious passers-by, increasing awareness like a kind of open-air art museum. Back in 1976, we trotted off to the only guesthouse nearby. A reluctant proprietor prised open a musty room. I spent a sleepless night.

Next morning, I introduced myself to Fateh, the wildlife warden for the park. He looked over his luxuriant moustache disbelievingly at me and my camera. No one came here, he told me, to 'visit'. Jolting along dirt tracks, we drove out towards the reserve. Slowly the wilderness took over. I scanned the thickening forest for wildlife, unaware my tracking skills would take years to develop.

My first days felt like shedding one layer of skin and growing into another. As you track a tiger, the language of the jungle envelopes you in its folds. You're alert to the tension in every rustling leaf, in every impression on the ground. Animal tracks whisper stories of the night. You're a jungle detective seeking clues of tigers having padded past.

In the early years, just a paw-print was cause for celebration. There were still villages everywhere; human disturbance was high. Until the 1980s, there were few pictures of tigers in the wild. Even then tourism to the area was only just starting, driven by Fateh's determination to make Ranthambore the most important wildlife destination in the world. My pictures of tigers like Noon drew multitudes to the forests of Ranthambore, transforming the local economy. People in the area owed their improving prospects to Noon.

Noon had been a tigress who filled my senses. Fateh teased me – saying I'd fallen in love with a tigress. Whenever I arrived in her presence there was a quick look of recognition. Most of the time it was just her and me with my camera. Visiting research-scientists warned me to keep detached, not humanise tigers, but Noon grew into a pleasant obsession, deepening my understanding of the secret life of tigers. I don't think I experienced such closeness with a tiger again.

> Commented [JL68]: Question 2- People and animals and how they have contributed

Back then I could drive out alone and watch tigers in solitude. There were fewer rules, fewer visitors asking to join me.

Even today, traversing the lakes which were at the heart of her territory, I can summon up images of Noon slicing through their waters or erupting from a grassy bank in incredible pursuits of deer or wild boar – images that remain etched on my mind.

Sometimes when hunting, Noon would look skywards and follow the direction vultures took. Visitors are still fascinated today by film of her tracking low-flying vultures, trotting from lake to lake until she found the carcass of a deer.

Back then, I explain, Ranthambore was full of white-backed vultures, before chemicals used for injecting livestock and ingested by these scavenging birds wiped them out. Nature lost a cleaning service. Noon lost her food-finders. I last saw Noon in 1990 beside Ranthambore lake. She looked older. Tigers get paler with age. The sun was setting, its last rays framing her in golden light. By this time, she'd successfully raised two litters and delighted the world with our footage of her kills, racing into the shallows of the lakes, causing chaos amongst grazing deer and more often than not bringing one down. The tourist boom followed – thanks to Noon – with no shortage of high-profile visitors keen to promote the cause of wild tigers.

> Commented [JL69]: Question 2 - Animals and exciting experiences

> Commented [JL70]: Question 3 How has Sawai Madhopur changed?

You are Fateh. Following the release of Val's book about his experiences at Ranthambore and the work you have both been doing there, you are interviewed for a national television show.

The interviewer asks you the following three questions only:

- What does Ranthambore offer visitors; what might our viewers like about Ranthambore if they visited **and** what sort of thing could they do there?

- Can you tell us about the various different people and animals associated with Ranthambore **and** how you feel they and you have contributed to Ranthambore's success?

Write the words of the interview. Base your interview on what you have read in **Text C**, but be careful to use your own words. Address each of the three bullets.

Begin your interview with the first question.

Write about 250 to 350 words.

Up to 15 marks are available for the content of your answer, and up to 10 marks for the quality of your writing

Interviewer: What does Ranthambore offer visitors; what might our viewers like about Ranthambore if they visited and what sort of thing could they do there?

> **Commented [JL71]:** Do not change the questions as opposed to a normal interview where the interviewer would start with a greeting.

Fateh: It is indeed an absolute pleasure to be interviewed by you. Well, Ranthambore is a treasure trove of natural beauty and wildlife experiences. What visitors find most captivating is the chance to witness the majestic tigers in their natural habitat. Our tiger reserve offers a unique blend of adventure and serenity. The sprawling landscapes, dotted with lakes and ancient ruins, provide a picturesque setting for wildlife enthusiasts and nature lovers. Visitors can embark on thrilling safaris, exploring the diverse flora and fauna, including various species of birds, deer, and the elusive leopards.

Beyond the wildlife, Ranthambore has a rich history with ancient forts and temples that add a cultural dimension to the visit. The ruins tell stories of a bygone era, creating a fascinating backdrop to the wilderness. For those seeking a more immersive experience, we encourage interactions with the local communities to understand their symbiotic relationship with the park.

> **Commented [JL72]:** Richness of language, punctuation and vocabulary, describing the attractions in detail

Interviewer: Now, could you tell us about the various different people and animals associated with Ranthambore and how you feel they and you have contributed to Ranthambore's success?

Fateh: Certainly! Ranthambore's success is a collective effort of dedicated individuals and the vibrant wildlife that calls this place home. The local communities have played a crucial role in conservation efforts, understanding the delicate balance between human activities and the preservation of nature. Val, the narrator of the book, has been a pivotal force in bringing international attention to Ranthambore through his photography and documentaries. His work has not only elevated the park's status but has also contributed significantly to local livelihoods through increased tourism.

Interviewer: Ranthambore is located near SM. How and why has SM changed since 1976?

Around 1976, Ranthambore was a very remote place with primitive infrastructure -hardly any guest houses or sprawling modes of transport. However, tigers like Noon have become iconic symbols of Ranthambore's success story and its development too. Through Val's lens, Noon and others have become ambassadors for global tiger conservation.

The collaboration between park authorities, conservationists, and the local communities has been instrumental in creating a sustainable model for wildlife preservation. Sawai Madhopur has been getting the buzz especially after 1980 and is one of the most popular sanctuaries now.

CHAPTER 8

ARTICLE WRITING

Articles, both magazine articles and news articles are asked in IGCSE English. The intent of writing an article is normally to provide key information as well as strongly persuade the reader. The articles posed in the exam are commonly asked in Paper 2 which is a more elaborate task and the marks too are higher compared to Paper 1.

The article pattern is specific and contains individual bullets to focus on such as putting forward different opinions, ideas and perspectives mentioned in the texts and then expressing your own opinion. The manner in which one should express their ideas will be dependent on key questions such as:

1. Who are you writing for? (Target audience) – Obviously, the language register and style should be according to the audience. For instance, if one is writing a magazine article for a young audience, the tone shouldn't be too formal or with too many jargons.
2. What should you write? (Focus on the information related to bullet points and paraphrase it and present in a very convincing and appealing manner.
3. How are you going to write it (Language style, tone, register etc)

Key tips for writing a very persuasive article:

1. Utilise all the elements of the 'A FOREST' Paradigm:

    A- Use of powerful and relevant adjectives and adverbs but also alliteration for the title or somewhere in the body paragraphs to create a rhetorical impact.

    F- Facts but also the fallacies or the drawbacks as a part of the various views, attitudes and approaches mentioned in the texts.

    0- Opinions is a significant element of an IGCSE article and should be expressed strongly and articulately.

R- Rule of three (Repeating words thrice for better effect) and Rhetorical Questions

E- Emotive language, appealing to pathos and ethos.

S- Statistics (Use of data, numbers or evidence such as expert testimonies etc).

T- Talking to your reader, use of personal pronouns to engage your audience and not excessively using too formal tone, instead more relatable vocabulary and writing style.

2. Use of more dramatic vocabulary and exaggeration or hyperbole.
3. Insert rhetorical questions in the first paragraph.
4. The article should have a catchy headline and a byline mentioning journalist or reporter's name.
5. The introduction should be compelling.

For example, writing an article about climate change can be started as follows:

Are we not the real culprits of climate change? The ongoing perils of industrialisation, pollution and population explosion have pushed us in the deep end.

1. The body paragraphs should be 3-4 mentioning facts, opinions and attitudes backed by evidence.
2. Connectors indicating continuation of ideas or parallelism of thoughts or contradictions should be used such as:

   Continuation – In addition, Along with, As well as

   Parallelism- Also, Similarly, Likewise, Identically

   Contradiction- Despite, However, Inspite of
6. Conclusion should summarise your point of view and perspectives.

Sample Task-

The key points of both the texts are marked as follows:

Text A: Can the world be saved from over-tourism?

We've officially entered the era of too much tourism. Sand has been removed by tourists from famous beaches and some cities impose fines on weary tourists just for sitting down in crowded hotspots. As local people fear being priced out of their towns and cities, stringent rules and limitations are imposed on holiday rentals. In Thailand, one popular destination has been closed indefinitely to allow its ecosystem to recover from the millions of tourists who have visited over recent years. Tourism taxes are becoming more common and, in some areas, are being used to restrict access to all but the wealthier clientele.

In a recent forum, tourism experts said that over-tourism was real: 'The overcrowding on the streets, the rising rents, the hostility of residents – they can't be denied.'

Over-tourism takes different forms in different places. In European cities, the over-crowding and pressure on resources, such as energy, water and health services, are obvious, but in many countries across the globe too many people are trying to gain access to fragile landscapes, buildings and ancient monuments.

In Iceland, the situation is different. 'The growth has been very fast,' explained the country's head of tourism. She was quick to clarify there are advantages to this tourism boom. Iceland's economy has been transformed. 'It's improved our lives. We enjoy a wider range of services and we can fly to more destinations.'

But pressure on popular tourist sites leaves environmental damage and changes people's attitudes. Social media plays a role and brings challenges

Commented [JL73]: Bullet 1- Type of view about tourism

Commented [JL74]: Bullet 1 - Negative attitude of the locals towards tourists due to over tourism

Commented [JL75]: Evidence that can be used to highlight Bullet no 1

Commented [JL76]: Other opinions and drawbacks- Bullet 1 and 2. Can be used to suggest to young people to not exert much load on the tourist places and their systems.

Commented [JL77]: Contrasting view (positive view) about role of tourism in certain places.

and opportunities. Iceland's landscape attracts attention, with hot springs and dramatic landscapes. 'Some celebrity puts out a selfie and suddenly hundreds start visiting some remote waterfall that isn't ready for the numbers.

It can be difficult to manage expectations.'

> Commented [JL78]: Bullet point 2 - What should youngsters not do in these popular or exotic places.

Over-tourism impacts housing and the lives of local people and does not always bring benefits. Tourists in big groups visit some of the oldest places in the world, using companies that don't share their wealth with local communities. That creates conflict with the population because they consider that tourist hotspot to be theirs. 'That's their own culture, their own ancestors and they get no benefit,' said one expert.

> Commented [JL79]: Bullet 1- Opinions about negative impacts of over tourism

Text B is taken from a magazine article about living in a famous tourist destination.

In the summer, Paolo Santini shares his hometown with three million temporary residents. A cultured man, Paolo has worked for 40 years in the city's museum, curating the region's ancient treasures exhibited for the visitors. Indeed, the day I interviewed him the museum was packed with weary families wandering aimlessly through Paolo's beloved artefacts.

> Commented [JL80]: Evidence about the extent of overtourism. Can be used in the introductory paragraphs.

'I was born here,' he says, 'in what was a rural backwater a few miles away. My father had a small farm and eked out a living, but it was tourism that gave me my profession and a decent standard of living. A lot of money has gone into making this city a popular destination.'

> Commented [JL81]: Positive view about tourism as per the person's testimony

He owns a modest house on the outskirts of the city, in what used to be a fishing village where his ancestors sold their catch on the beach. It's become a popular area in recent years for summer

Article Writing

homes for those who live elsewhere most of the year. Paolo says the summers are difficult for locals. The traffic is suffocating, and the pavements are crowded and hot. 'At least the city's facilities are open all year now. Everything used to close in the winter. Most of the cultural events and festivals are still organised around the visitors. We've spent decades "improving the visitor experience", as they say.' Paolo betrays only a hint of irony.

> **Commented [JL82]:** Irony surrounding over crowding and challenges due to too many tourists

The city's central squares are lined with cramped, packed cafes and restaurants, which make me question the visitors' experience. Local shops have been bought up and converted to cafes and souvenir shops. 'There are no chemists or butchers left in the centre now and the rents are sky high,' says Paolo.

> **Commented [JL83]:** Bullet 2- Things which young people can consider before visiting too common places ,cafes

His adult son lives at home, unable to afford his own house. There are rumblings of more organised discontent, with residents' groups resisting further incursions of tourism or the rising costs of living in a city they no longer recognise as theirs.

> **Commented [JL84]:** Local cons about economy and growing discontent of locals.

Paolo is ambivalent: 'This city has given me a good life, better than I could have expected as a child. In my line of work, cultural exchange between people is good and tourism can expand all our horizons. But I hope we know how and when to put the brakes on it.'

> **Commented [JL85]:** Confounding view about tourism being advantageous on one side but should not over do it.

Write an article for young people, advising them what they need to consider when deciding on a holiday destination.

In your article you should:

- evaluate the ideas, opinions and attitudes in both texts
- suggest what young people should consider in order to make a responsible decision.

Base your article on what you have read in both texts, but be careful to use your own words.

Address both of the bullet points.

Write about 250 to 350 words.

Up to 15 marks are available for the content of your answer, and up to 25 marks for the quality of your writing.

Sample Answer:

The Bane of Overtourism and How to be a Conscious Traveller.

By- Dr. Jyuthica Laghate

Throughout the globe, tourists are exploring an array of places, both common and exotic from Iceland to the heart of Europe, from Disneyland to South east Asia. Ironically, overtourism is a real phenomenon having lot of adverse and far-reaching impacts on the local ecosystem, environment and overall attitude of the locals towards the tourists. As expressed gravely by one of the residents, Paolo Santini, "We must know how and when to put the brakes on it."

Firstly, most of the renowned tourist attractions have been affected to a large extent due to overcrowding, excessive footfall and major destruction of the natural landscape. As young people, it is completely warranted to travel but you have to be very vigilant, responsible and accountable for the scenic place that you fancy.

It must be understood that there are so many issues that arise when people travel in humungous numbers to beaches or places where there are ancient monuments. Most of the sand of the beaches or these ancient structures can get seriously impacted or destroyed because of too much human consumption.

Additionally, the locals become quite hostile to this heavy influx of outsiders and correspondingly the holiday rental prices increase exponentially. The other hazards are too much of traffic congestion, heat and suffocation. Hence, be prudent while choosing your holiday destination.

Strong antagonizing views have been expressed about overtourism taking a toll on local energy, health and electricity bills and even housing rents. Cities are becoming virtually impossible to afford living in and so many local communities have put forth their severe discontentment.

On the other hand, there are certain unique holiday destinations such as Iceland, wherein the local economy has been boosted and they look forward to more tourists.

Sometimes, a tourist destination is randomly chosen on the basis of one celebrity selfie venturing a real remote corner which might not be even prepared for real tourism. If thousands and thousands of tourists flock here, it can definitely be a disaster. It is therefore wiser to choose destinations carefully in a way that does not disrupt the local serenity and environment.

Make sure, you don't overcrowd an already crammed place and do not unsettle the locales otherwise the experience might not be of an ideal holiday. Choosing the right season is also crucial. For example, in temperate places, all the facilities might be inadequate or closed during winter.

One of the other important concerns is booking with travel agents who might be predatory and who are not willing to share the profit with the local agents or communities. and therefore, one might not receive ideal welcome or impeccable customer service in the tourist destination.

Travelling in the current heyday can be daunting especially when the peace and bucolic surroundings of beautiful country side is overfilled with travellers. Therefore, one has to be cautious in rightly choosing the destination that can offer beautiful landscapes, great local cuisine and friendly vibe.

CHAPTER 9

WRITING A NEWS REPORT AND A FORMAL REPORT

Both News reports and Formal reports are asked in IGCSE English examination. There are certain similarities and differences in both these writing types.

The similarities are stated as follows:

1. Both these types provide information about the details of the event/project/ programme such as What was the event? Where it took place? When? Who were the key people? Why or the agenda? and How or the details of functioning?
2. The first two medium sized paragraphs in both news report and a formal report can include the aforementioned information.
3. The body paragraphs in both these forms can be 3 -4.
4. Both have a 5-6 paragraph structure.

The differences are:

1. The language style in news report is much more sensationalised and the tone is dramatic compared to a formal report which is way too formal and simplistic.
2. The word choices in a news report are much more flashy and catchy compared to a formal one wherein the word choices are restrained, official and measured.
3. Use of figurative devices such as alliteration, metaphors or hyperbole (exaggeration) is seen commonly in a news report while it is not prescribed for a formal report.
4. News reports have a mention of future events or possibilities while formal report has recommendations and suggestions but are strictly about the said task or activity.

5. Formal reports are more of practical or empirical tools for an organisation while news reports essential report key events in a prominent manner.

News reports:

As mentioned above, news reports present key events, happenings of various kinds in an extremely engaging and appealing manner. A news report should have an extremely gripping headline followed by a byline mentioning the reporter's name and the place where he or she is reporting from.

The introductory paragraph addressed the 4 W's and 1 H (What, When, Why, Where, How?). The body paragraphs include an elaboration of the key aspects of the news, its positive or negative facets in a much more dramatic and poignant (emotionally moving) manner. It also includes reporting key statistics, say for a sports report or certain expert testimonies or witness statements for crime reporting.

The conclusion includes a brief insight of future possibilities and some recommendations.

All the facets of the A FOREST paradigm for creating persuasive content can be effectively used such as vivid adjectives and adverbs, facts supported by statistics, use of rhetorical questions, repetition of emotive words and engaging readers with a relatable tone, as if the reporter is actually conversing with the reader.

Sample Task:

Imagine you are the journalist from the local newspaper at the meeting.

Write a newspaper report about the meeting.

In your newspaper report you should:

- describe the atmosphere and reactions of the crowd at the meeting
- give your impression of the two speakers and the arguments that they made
- suggest what you think might happen in the future.

Base your newspaper report on what you have read in Passage A, but be careful to use your own words. Address each of the three bullet points.

Begin your newspaper report: 'Yesterday the local community met together to debate a proposal which has implications for all of us…'

Write about 250 to 350 words.

Up to 15 marks are available for the content of your answer, and up to 5 marks for the quality of your writing.

Text:

A Common Land

Villagers meet to hear proposals from a large company wishing to develop a piece of common land. The crowd swarmed into the building, many eager to hear plans that might bring prosperity to their town. Others wore grim expressions, aware of the titanic fight needed to save a precious site. Anuja scanned the people, many roughly dressed and weather-beaten from long hours of working outdoors. None looked well-fed – except the main speaker, the representative of the development company. 'You know why we are here tonight,' a leading member of the community began. 'FoodFreight wants to build a depot on our common land next to the river. Mr Carmichael is here to tell us why we should let them.' The temperature in the room rose as the meeting wore on.

> **Commented [D86]:** Reactions of the crowd and the atmosphere
>
> **Commented [D87R86]:**

Hands were swept across sweaty brows and some removed outer garments. A short break was announced during which people could look at the glossy plans and maps pinned up around the hall, and enjoy cool drinks and delicious looking snacks thoughtfully provided by Food Freight. Fingers traced the lines of new roads on the maps. A journalist sought out Anuja and her companions. 'The company is just trying to bribe our people,' remarked Anuja. 'Not just with a few drinks but with a promise of a medical centre.' 'Yes,' added a man at her side. 'And I spoke to Dr Misha yesterday when she was here on her weekly visit. She said what we really need is a proper hospital, where operations can take place.' The meeting resumed.

Rufus Carmichael rose to speak. 'As you all know, the area bordering the river is an eyesore. What use is it to anyone? Tall trees cast heavy shade. Noxious weeds choke the ground. Indeed it is an impenetrable thicket, a haven for vermin, a lair for undesirables. And noisy rooks have taken over the canopy, with their raucous, unending cries. We will sweep this away. Your town will be a pleasanter place.' His voice boomed. Anuja clenched her fist and muttered, 'Those are ancient oaks. The rooks' nests are used by the red footed falcons, beautiful and rare birds!' She shook her head in disbelief.

Rufus was still talking, '…Warehouses will be built. The new harbour that we will build downstream will create a magnet for your local produce. Your market will overflow with food and will become a symbol of your new-found prosperity.' Anuja thought of the reliable supply of meat from the deer that fed on the acorns in the woodland, a bonus for local hunters. 'There could be jobs for many of you. And after we have developed the land, we will build a medical centre for you.' People squirmed in their seats, turning to neighbours to exchange excited comments. Anuja could stand it no longer. 'Sir,' she began, 'and my people: our ancestors began this settlement on that piece of land. They planted those majestic trees hundreds of years ago.' She strode to the front to address the people directly. 'Remember the stories your parents told you. If those trees die, our settlement will fall into decline. Yes, we have neglected it, but with the neglect has come increases in wildlife, even rare species of dragonflies and field mice.

We can carefully clear up the mess of weeds so it remains a home to the lovely creatures. We could resurrect the sacred rituals that used to take place here every year.' As Anuja expanded on the virtues of the site, ragged cheers went up, first from those sitting near her. The sound strengthened as people became again conscious of its many benefits. This was a special place!

Rufus' face tightened into a grimace. His lips had compressed into a thin line of anger. Dots of perspiration sprang out on his forehead. He banged his fist on the table to quieten the crowd. 'Gentlemen – and ladies – just listen to sense,' he began. Jeers and boos broke out. A dark cloud passed across his face, and suddenly he was panting as though he had run a race. His good humour was gone. 'My company is stronger than all of you!' he shouted. 'We will get our way!' Not long after this, the meeting broke up in some disarray. As Anuja and her friends left, a blue-grey falcon jetted across the skies, the red of its undertail and legs clearly visible. It swooped on a large insect, then veered away before heading for some treetops visible above the houses. Fat drops of rain began to fall, then lightning sizzled across the sky. A portent, perhaps.

> **Commented [D91]:** Heated reaction of Rufus

Sample Answer:

'Food Freight' Plans to Massacre the Village Landscape"-Will they Succeed?

By – Jyuthica Laghate

Yesterday's auspicious morning marked the historic meeting of the villagers of Vilaspur, who along with their strong representative, Anuja, gathered in humungous numbers to meet with the company head, Mr.Rufus Carmicahel, of the huge food corporation, Food Freight.

There was a lot of zeal, excitement as well as palpable anxiety on the part of villagers because at the end of the day, it was a matter of losing or retaining their ancestral, nature rife land by the riverside.

The gathering had gotten very animated, with so many people profusely sweating and waiting edgily for the result. Mr.Carmichael, in a very persuasive tone, described about the company's plans to enable real growth and development by scraping the so called 'unproductive land by the riverbed' and converting into a thriving harbour along with the facilities of warehouses, health care etc. In his words, "The new harbour will be a magnet for money", indeed reinforced his pure commercial interest in capturing the land.

In stark contrast, the villagers along with Anuja, passionately opposed this prospect by arguing that, the local landscape, although not maintained, is a house for rare and beautiful birds, insects and flies adding to the rustic beauty of the landscape. They were also extremely upset and impassioned about their ancestral legacy and nostalgia being crushed because of this industrial plan and were completely against it.

As expected, Mr. Carmichael was extremely agitated with these hostile reactions of the villagers and even strongly indicated that their company was powerful enough to uproot them or dictate terms. The atmosphere of the meeting was frenzied to the least.

What happens next would be very path breaking because it could be the win of the industrial giants or the common village folk who hold their land so near and dear. The pendulum has always oscillated towards the rich and the influential- let us see if that changes in this case.

Formal Report:

There are differences between a formal report and a news report as follows:

Language - Flashy, Flamboyant and Compelling in a news report while it is much more factual, simplistic and pragmatic in a formal report.

Tone - Hard hitting and catchy in a news report while in a formal report it is neutral and formal.

Similarities – The first paragraph of both these reports is similar as in both of them include key information about What was the event? When did it happen? Where? Why? And How?

The structure of a formal report can be summarised as follows:

1. Start the report by addressing to the receiver (CEO, Head, Manager etc.)
2. A simple title is expected.
3. The report can have a five-paragraph structure.
4. The introduction highlights the aims, objectives and the whereabouts.

5. (Answer the four W's as stated above and How?)
6. The body paragraphs can be three, with each paragraph including about 4-5 points related to the question. Key observations, facts and opinions are the pivotal parts of a body paragraph.
7. The conclusive paragraph is about effective recommendations or future initiatives.
8. The register should be formal and pragmatic with no room for exaggeration.
9. Precise and concise presentation of facts, evidence and opinions.
10. Use of powerful vocabulary and passive voice is the key.
11. Use of subheadings such as Insights, Highlights /Features and Recommendations before paragraphs.

Sample task:

Text C: Riding the rails: learning how to drive a dog-sled

In this article, journalist Lyn Marshall looks back at her adventure holiday in Alaska.

As the sky gradually turned indigo in the fading light, the scraping of ice and frantic unheeded commands to my sled dog-team broke the stillness. Thundering down the frozen waterway, I snatched anxious glimpses over my shoulder. Where was Mike, my guide? Would his tracker still pick up my signal with the gap between us increasing by the minute? Out exploring that Friday evening, an irresistible scent had wafted by my lead dog's keen nose.

Following primal instincts over my feeble instructions, he'd wheeled around, leading his obliging pack in the opposite direction at full speed! Applying all my weight to the hook brake saved me from fishtailing wildly from side to side but did nothing to slow the dogs' enthusiastic charge. From my evening chats with Mike over the last few days, I knew that if we lost each other entirely, I was in trouble. I had nothing – no extra clothing, no shelter, but more importantly, nothing to start a fire. We'd seen wolf tracks regularly, so fire seemed particularly important to me at that moment. * * *

It was March, the tail end of the long, cold winter. Roads were closed, rivers were frozen, and access into the region was limited. Still spellbound from gazing at the enormity of the Alaskan wilderness, I'd stepped down from the mail-plane into the miniature perfection of Eagle, a fascinating, history-packed hamlet of timber dwellings, home to just 85 residents. I was immediately wrapped in the customary bear hug by Mike's wife, Scarlett, and cocooned in layers of Arctic-grade outerwear.

Scarlett live sustainably, hunting, fishing and gathering, consciously leaving a minimal carbon footprint. They've enjoyed many years of wilderness expeditions using traditional dog-sleds and now provide opportunities for adventurous souls to experience their eco-lifestyle first hand. Driving a dog-sled is harder than it looks. As Mike's passenger, I realised it involved constant corrective manoeuvres anticipating the dog-team's next move (they only ever do what they want to) and possible camber (tilt in the trail).

In theory lessons, Mike's diagrams emphasised that the 'ice highway' can be anything from porcelain smooth to oversized ice cubes (slam into one of those and you'd need your emergency messaging device), but winding through spruce forests tracing soft, snow-covered lines is a precious delight. Criss-crossing a small lake's glassy surface, I looked down to see exquisite designs – crystal bubbles of all shapes and sizes suspended in time, cascading into the dark depths. There were, of course, many thrills and spills. Losing control on one adrenalin-charged downhill run, I tipped sideways onto the snow. My happy, yappy team continued on, their inept operator hanging on single-handedly, thankful for the padded trousers provided. Each evening, we settled in at a different location, often an old miner's cabin, where our teams were secured and cared for. The teams are your lifeline, your escape route, so their health and wellbeing are paramount. Only after this did we collect snow for our water and cut firewood. The most memorable night?

Using only nature's materials, we shovelled and hacked, creating a shelter against the sub-zero temperature. A reflective wall of logs threw the pit-fire's heat under our makeshift roof as Mike spoke with passion about life out here, the joy of relative freedom and the Aurora Borealis in the night skies that were

nature's artwork: a ceiling of stars on dark nights, or flooded with rippling, emerald green curtains.

As I burrowed down for the night, fire crackling in the stillness, the howling of wolves drifted to us. It was a moment of complete and utter contentment. * * * Exactly how far I travelled through the twilight with my errant team, I'll never know. Our detour didn't have a dramatic end in the fangs of a wolf pack. Only when fatigued did the team slow, gliding to a halt with Mike rounding the bend sometime later to locate me.

Sample task:

You are Mike. The Ultimate Experience Travel Company which advertises your expeditions has seen Lyn Marshall's article reviewing her holiday in Alaska and has some concerns about the expedition and about using dogs to pull sleds. The company has asked you for a formal report.

In your report you should:

- explain exactly what happened during the evening exploration and the measures you take to ensure the safety and comfort of tourists
- remind the company of the different things tourists enjoy about the holiday you offer and why
- reassure the company that its various concerns about using dogs to pull sleds are unfounded and explain why you think that this form of transport is important to protect. Write the words of the report Write about 250–350 words. Up to 15 marks are available for the content of your answer and up to 10 marks for the quality of your writing.

Sample Answer:

To

The Head,

The Ultimate Experience Travel Company.

A report on tourist's concerns about the dog sled expedition and measures undertaken

By- Mr. Mike.

Insights

In one of our recent dog sled expeditions in Alaska, there was one member, Lyn Marshall, who was particularly concerned about some misadventure that occurred whilst being on the dog sled. Unpredictably, the dog sniffed a distinct smell and randomly went in that direction as a result of which, it was unsettling and frightening for Lyn. Also, there was a certain gap between me and Lynn due to which she was slightly more anxious.

It is frequently common that the dog sleds are not very static or typically balanced modes of transport but that is the hallmark of an adventurous Alaskan expedition and it would be fair to state that the tourists were formally informed about the nature of the icy roads, steep gradients and all the possible challenges that could ensue.

Highlights

As a sustainable, travel enterprise, my wife and I made sure we welcomed Lynn particularly with a friendly hug and ensured she had the most protective and relevant Arctic gear and felt cosy. As an extension of our nature friendly lifestyle comprising of hunting, fishing and gathering, we provide all these opportunities under safety measures to all our tourists/passengers.

Although, consumers like Lynn have expressed some concerns about the expedition, the stunning wilderness and the experiences certainly outweigh the perceived dangers. For instance, the beautiful cascading ice balls, ice laden roads forming transparent and stunning formations, using nature's reserves to subsist such as snow melted water and firewood amidst drifting wolves, certainly is no ordinary experience. The safety of everyone is ensured by resorting to so many varied and fascinating shelters such as old miners cabins, jungle stops etc.

Recommendations

The very essence of such kind of tourist experience should entail utmost use of natural and sustainable experiences and therefore use of dog sleds completely fulfils that need. Also, the possible dangers are not so marked as highlighted and hence use of dog sleds as an exciting mode of transport should be encouraged and not abandoned.

CHAPTER 10

WRITERS EFFECT

Writer's effect question is a long form question asked in Paper 1 and carries 15 marks. The expected word limit is 200-300 words. The aim of the question is to test student's explicit as well as implicit understanding of:

- What is the obvious meaning and the implied meaning of the powerful words and phrases that the author has used to convey his thoughts effectively and impactfully.
- How the author has used various language devices such as vivid vocabulary, figures of speech or writing style as tools to convey the messages in a highly appealing manner.
- What is the effect that the author is trying to create through his word choices, language style, tone and register.

One of the simplest ways of excelling in this question are to focus on the following points:

1. The first and foremost thing is to choose the evidence or the the words and phrases that are extremely powerful, evocative and figurative in the mentioned paragraphs to elaborate the writer's effect.

   Tip: Choosing phrases is easier and productive because one can explain a lot in detail as well as maintain a sizeable length.
2. The second thing is to write an in-depth explanation of the explicit meaning, the implicit or the hidden meaning of the phrase/word.
3. The third vital step is to focus on how the author has conveyed the meaning using language devices.

4. The fourth step is to express the kind of effect that the writer has tried to generate on the audience and how has that been done. (Using figurative devices, dramatic sentences, a certain tone etc.)

The structure of a writer's effect answer is as follows:

1. Commence the write-up by explaining what the overall topic of the passage and what the writer is conveying.
2. Focus now on the specific phrases or words and offer relevant explanation about their meanings, the tools that the author has used to convey the meaning such as imagery and other figurative devices, etc.
3. Also, comment on the overall effect of the phrases that the writer is trying to induce.

Sample Task:

Re-read paragraphs 9 and 10.

- Paragraph 9 begins 'From inside ' and is about the first evening in the lodge.
- Paragraph 10 begins 'Next morning' and is about meeting the wolves.

Explain how the writer uses language to convey meaning and to create effect in these paragraphs. Choose three examples of words or phrases from each paragraph to support your answer. Your choices should include the use of imagery.

Write about 200 to 300 words.

Up to 15 marks are available for the content of your answer.

Annotation:

From inside the plush mountain lodge, I've been promised a view of the Northern Lights. I peer out of the large viewing windows. As my eyes

> **Commented [D92]:** Plush indicates that the lodge despite being situated at a height and remote place such as a mountain was still luxurious, comfortable and remarkable to stay.

adjust to the night, I see a green glow: at first just smudges that grow, forming a cosmic phantom that flutters, swirls and moves mysteriously across the vast sky. Surfacing from the depths of the darkness we hear a sudden, vicious wolf-fight. 'Siblings working out their hierarchy,' says Stig casually. 'We don't interfere.'

We finish dinner in eerie silence, gazing at a shimmering white moon – silhouetted against it are the swift shadows of running wolves.

Next morning, emboldened by a hearty breakfast, Stig and I venture out and immediately spot the wolf pack loping eagerly towards us. They jump up excitedly, licking our faces. Two of them have a snarling stand-off over who should lick me first but then agree to lick my camera instead. Apart from that one moment, it's all remarkably non-threatening. We stroll to a low snow-covered hill where they do a bit of a howl and hold a wrestling contest. Only when I drop my phone is there a sudden intimation of what can happen. They are instantly curious and pushy, flooded with predatory instincts and the power of the pack. Moving slowly, I retrieve my phone and retreat to a respectful distance. Cute they may be, but cuddly toys they are not.

Commented [D93]: Green glow indicating a mysterious ray of light that merely taints the dark sky adding that layer of anticipation, anxiety and intrigue.

Commented [D94]: The phrase highlights the creation of a bizzare, ghostlike image or shadow in the sky that complete makes the reader apprehensive, nervous and tries to create an atmosphere of spookiness or some kind of alien encounter.

Commented [D95]: The wolf fight almost comes too randomly or as a shock to them expecially in that sheer darkness and it is pretty hardcore and brutal and therefore quite frightening.

Commented [D96]: Emboldened here implies that the visitor and the guide, Stig had a sumptuous breakfast and were completely energized and vitalized because of it. They were now all ready to face the day's adventure with all that vigour

Commented [D97]: The pack of wolves was kind of keenly rushing towards the writer and Stig creating the feeling of being vulnerable, and extreme uncertainty and danger.

Commented [D98]: Author has adeptly used Alliteration here to create the lasting impact of wolves howling and fighting to their teeth with each other to strangely get a chance to lick these two fondly.

Commented [D99]: Ironically they look furry and cuddly but they are too fierce, attacking and secretive when it comes to attacking people suddenlu.

Sample Answer:

As a whole, Paragraph 9 throws light on the writer's mixed experience of staying in the mountain lodge, wherein he is all looking forward to see the magical Northern Lights but at the same time, the pitch black darkness, freezing climate and the whole terrifying vibe unsettles him. Through the distinct usage of the word, "plush", the author has highlighted a very peculiar aspect of the lodge being luxurious, comfortable and pleasurable despite being a mountain lodge at such a height and remoteness.

The phrase, "forming a cosmic phantom" very evocatively highlights the streak of light creating bizzare and frightening ghost like or spooky image hovering in the dark sky. This visual imagery creates a feeling of deep fright, anticipation, anxiety and mystery as to what is going to be in store next. The quotation, "sudden, vicious wolf fight", further adds to the apprehension and potential danger where the writer and the guide, Steg, hear wolves fighting to their teeth, aggressively and that could mean, these two guys are in a complete impasse or a point of no return.

In a nutshell, Paragraph 10, talks at length about the writer's encounter with the wolves and the extreme unpredictability yet utter thrill associated with that. The inventive use of vocabulary such as "emboldened" explicates that the writer and the guide had a sumptuous, wholesome breakfast due to which they felt very energised and vitalised. They were now all ready and full of vigour to face the adventure that the day was going to throw at them.

Through the phrase, "snarling stand-off", the author has utilised powerful auditory imagery by denoting the exact snarling or howling sound of the wolves that was heard and the writer has also used Alliteration figuratively to add further impact of the whole encounter as more fierce, threatening and brutal. There is also an interesting contrast here, since the wolves were actually haggling to lick these two fondly but that too was so frightful.

Through the quote, "But, cuddly they are not", the author has used the connector ,'but' ,to its optimum effect by emphasising that the wolves being furry and all might seem adorable and cuddly but they are actually one of the most unpredictable, raging predators who might attack anytime and hence maintaining a safe distance is the best move.

CHAPTER 11

DESCRIPTIVE WRITING

*D*escriptive writing is one of the vital questions in Paper 2 (Directed Writing and Composition). It is a long form question carrying highest weightage of 40 marks.

What exactly is Descriptive writing in IGCSE?

The question may sound bizarre but it is crucial in order to plan descriptive writing in the most perfect and expected manner for the finals.

Right from Key Stage 2, descriptive writing is introduced and is actually one of the predictable and feasible tasks as far as achieving high scores and excellence is concerned.

Descriptive writing is essentially a detailed or in-depth description of the time, place, events, characters, experiences, things and contexts that the author represents or delivers.

The fundamental purpose of descriptive writing is to describe a person, place, event, experience, thoughts, feelings or actions in the most vivid and expressive manner. The whole intent is to literally create an exact picture of the person, place, thing or event in the mind of the reader. The primary idea is create an extremely catchy, engaging and powerful piece.

It is different from narrative writing in the sense that it does not create a new character or a motive but explains an event, occurrence, person or a place in a most detailed and appealing manner and evoking all the senses of the reader.

Hence, the whole approach is to 'Show' or 'Demonstrate explicitly' and not merely 'Tell' or 'Express'.

Some of the principal rules that should be kept in mind while attempting descriptive writing are as follows:

1. **Effective use of sensory words is essential, that is, words appealing to all the five senses such as sight, hearing, smell, taste and touch.**

These words can exactly create the effect of the experience, place, person or thing in terms of what is seen, felt, heard, smelt or tasted.

Sensory words:

1. Appealing to sight – various colours, sizes and shapes.

   For e.g. the turquoise blue waves, the gigantic ship, the roughly circular whirlpool.

2. Appealing to hearing – various sounds, pleasant and unpleasant.

   For e.g. Cracking of the door, roaring of the wind, music of the trees, songs of the birds carefully orchestrated.

3. Appealing to taste – focussing on various types of taste. For e.g. excessively sweet chocolate, brackish water, sour orange, tangy soup.

4. Appealing to smell –appealing to a range of smells from fragrant to foul. For e.g. foul, balmy, fragrant, fishy, piquant and ambrosial.

5. Appealing to touch- various aspects of touch such as blunt, rough, blemished, blistered, rough, jagged, smooth, soft as silk, cushioned, lacerated, hit harshly.

2. **Employing potent vocabulary especially impactful adjectives, verbs and adverbs.**

For example,

While describing a place, if you say, 'The place is nice', the impact is limited whereas, if you express, 'The place is absolutely spectacular and one of its kind with its expansive beaches and plethora of flora and fauna', the adjectives and adverbs here really create that strong impact on the audience which is one of the pivotal attributes of an effective descriptive essay.

3. **Use of figurative devices adds to the quality of portrayal and creates a deeper appeal.**

It just does not create a literal effect but helps to make the portrayal layered, rich and articulate.

For e.g. figures of speech such as Imagery, Simile, Metaphor, Oxymoron, Antithesis, Personification, Exaggeration or Hyperbole, Alliteration, Onomatopoeia, Climax and so many others can be utilised effectively and create an everlasting effect.

4. **Effective use of punctuation such as semi-colons, colons, commas and exclamations is important. Also use of single dashes to introduce shocking or surprising pieces of information is vital.**

For example, The forbidden forest was haunted – sinister and bleak. In this instance, the single dash introduces a key and shocking piece of information.

5. **Focussing on different times within a day or a season or contrasting information adds to the depth of information.**

For instance, the description of a lake during sunrise and sunset.

The sun casted his brilliance upon the serene water in the east or The setting sun lays his black cloak over the shimmering white water by twilight.

Focus on how different times within a day add to striking pieces of expression.

6. **The writing should be such that it enhances the imagination of the readers. Therefore, use of imagery is central to a well penned descriptive piece.**

Imagery is of five types like sensory words. The five types are visual imagery, auditory imagery, olfactory imagery, gustatory imagery and kinesthetic imagery.

7. **Varying the sentence structure like using some shorter sentence fragments, some question tags etc adds to the effect.**

8. **The description should not be static but progressive and lead the reader through an experience such as passing or travelling through time points or going specifically through a period of time such as one particular hour and describe that with minute details.**

9. **Different paragraphs can include additional details or contrasting information.**

Tips about describing a person, place, event or an experience.

1. Describing a person-
    a. Mention in detail about the person's physical appearance, specifically about whether he is tall, short, chubby, lanky, thin or overweight, obese.

b. Explicitly describe about the unique characteristics of his physical features, whether he/she has a short or excessively pointed nose, fair or dark complexion, with or without blemishes or a scar.

c. Simple things such as the colour of the hair, the kind of haircut also add meaningful bits to the description.

d. One can use key elements such as his/her beaming smile or a strange smirk or simply an understated change of expression.

e. The next important facets are his/her personality types whether an optimistic, simple, genuine personality, a humble, helpful soul or slightly crooked, wry or severely intolerant, strict task master or a malevolent, evil person. Several shades of personality add to the depth of the description.

f. The other elements are about the behaviour and communication of the person with his family, colleagues, for instance whether he is a loner, introvert or highly social, personable etc.

For example- *Sarah was a beaming, nineteen year old girl with Disneyland dreams and twinkling brown eyes. Her ginger hair added to her earthy persona and she was the apple of everyone's eye in school. Her pretty heart matched her pretty looks. She would often come singing and humming her favourite songs and would lighten up a room. Her talks were as long as sticks but her voice as gentle and musical like a cuckoo.*

The paragraph describes in detail her physical appearance in terms of her smile, her eyes, her hair, her beaming and cheerful nature and her soft, melodious voice. This detailed depiction adds to the quality and impact of the portrayal.

2. **Describing a place :** While describing a place,
    a. Talk about the exact location, whether it is urban, semi-urban or rural
    b. Describe its peculiar features whether picturesque, excessively polluted, a peaceful, idyllic countryside or a mystical, forbidden forest.
    c. Use figurative devices such as Personification, Simile, Metaphor, Onomatopoeia or Oxymoron in explaining the sounds and strange attributes of the non-living elements and how they personify human actions .For e.g. the moaning wind, the cluttering door, the scare of the

leaves getting crushed on the ground, the darkness of the forest as terrifying as the hidden monster etc.

d. When describing a place of tourist interest, say in a tourist blog or article, describe how far the place is from your house (how you got there) and why did you like the place?

e. Describe the unique features of the place and its specialities?

f. Describe the weather and how it felt "hot" or "cold", sweaty or airy, caught up or liberating when you were there.

g. Would you recommend the place to others (for vacations, etc.)? If yes, then why?

For example, a pristine beach in an exotic place like Maldives can be described as below:

The bellowing turquoise blue waves with a diaphanous bottom replete with corals seemed to wash out all the sorrows out of my mind. The white sands were as soft as the chalk falling exquisitely, getting soaked and ideally prepared for building long tall castles. The dense shrubs and coating of coconut trees with luscious coconuts hanging in the grooves created a perfect green landscape in contrast with the ethereal sky, meeting the sea at several points creating the best embellished necklace of nature's blue sapphire.

3. Describe a thing – Important points for writing a convincing description of a thing are as follows:

a. Describe the dimensions, size, shape, colour, if it is a branded thing, the specialities of the brand.

b. What place does the thing hold in your heart?

Describe a piece of jewellery that is your prized possession.

The small streak of diamonds interspersed in between the central large emerald pendant still sits tall in the cold attic. The piece of jewellery is emblematic of the surreal joys of the wedding day and the huge wedding gift received from my husband. The lustrous gleam from the diamonds provide a new hope and spirit and light up any event or a state of mind. The middle humungous green, seamlessly oval pendant anoints the whole necklace like a sacred deity looking after its devotees through the thick and thin. The necklace is tailor made for my neck and the voice of my persona within, free and uninhibited.

Figurative devices useful for descriptive writing:

1. Imagery:

Imagery utilises sensory words and descriptions to appeal to the reader's five senses as well as his/her internal thoughts and sentiments.

Like the five senses, Imagery is of five types such as Visual imagery(creating visual pictures), Auditory imagery(creating sounds), Gustatory imagery(creating tastes), Olfactory imagery(creating smells) and Kinesthetic imagery(appealing to sense of touch or pressure.

E.g. The orchestrated songs of the cuckoo woke us up to this golden sun shining brilliantly and made us sense the divine music of nature, the humming of the bees, the mellifluous voices of the birds and the gentle stream of the turquoise water calming us from within. We were now ready for an aromatic breakfast, exotic fruits, shining red and green against the hitting of the steel cutlery.

The words divine music, orchestrated, humming, mellifluous and hitting create the sense of those different sounds.

The words golden sun, shining red and green create a vivid sense of colour and appearance The words aromatic create a sense of pleasant smell.

2. Simile:

Simile is comparing two things by using the words **like, such as, as** etc.

Similes can be used to the fullest in descriptive write ups to add clarity and vibrancy to the things compared. Comparing things always adds to the relevance and relatability.

For instance, while describing a person, one can say, 'He was as intrepid as a lion' meaning he was as brave as the lion or 'The little girl's face was glowing like the refulgent moon' meaning the girl's face was glowing like the shining or brilliant moon.

3. Metaphor:

Metaphors also add a layer of depth and relatability to an interpretation. Metaphor is calling one thing as the other without using words such as 'like', 'such as', 'as' etc.

Let us say, 'Lily was a diamond in her own regard' meaning she had some special qualities and was valuable.

4. Oxymoron and Anti-thesis:

Oxymoron introduces two contrasting words in the same phrase while Anti-thesis introduces contrasting words in a sentence but not in the same phrase or side by side.

For instance, She heard the pleasantly deafening voice is an Oxymoron where pleasantly and deafening are conflicting words in the same phrase while

United we stand, divided we fall is an Anti-thesis wherein the two opposite words, united and divided are used in the sentence but not in the same phrase.

The use of Oxymoron or Anti-thesis heightens the contrast in the description and makes it more layered and deep.

5. Onomatopoeia:

Using words that convey the sound and the actual meaning of the word through the sounds.

Appealing to the sense of hearing is one of the important factors of creating a vivid description and Onomatopoeia helps immensely in that regard. For e.g. words like cluttering, thundering, crushing, jangling etc convey the meaning with their sounds.

6. Alliteration:

Alliteration is used extensively in descriptive or narrative writing to enable the write-up to be more catchy and impactful since it is repetition of sounds.

Alliteration is of different types as follows:

A. Assonance- **Assonance** is the repetition of vowel sounds (a, e, i, o, u).

    E.g. Try to light the fire- Repetition of 'i' sound.

B. Consonance- **Consonance** is the repetition of consonant sounds (sounds or letters apart from vowels).

E.g. She struck a stroke of bad luck -Repetition of 's' sound.

C. Sibilance- **Sibilance** is the repetition of hissing's' sounds (s, c and sometimes z, f, v)

E.g., The snake went forward, hissing and spitting, slithering on her scaly bottom.

6. Personification, Pathetic fallacy and Anthropomorphism –

Personification is about giving human qualities to non-human things such as plants, animals or objects.

For example, The wind was howling like never before.

Anthropomorphism is about giving human form or human parts/organs to non-human things such as plants, animals or objects. The word anthropomorphism is derived from two words, 'anthropo' meaning human and 'morphism' meaning change in form or structure.

For example, The tree spoke faintly from the bottom of her throat.

Pathetic fallacy is similar to Personification but it mainly refers to giving human emotions, mood or mournful characters to the nature or weather to set the tone of the material.

For example, The rain was weeping like never before.

7. Inversion

Inversion is a figure of speech wherein the usual order of words in a sentence is reversed. For e.g., Gone were the emotions and the joy instead of saying, 'The emotions and joy were gone.'

8. Climax

Climax is a figure of speech in which the words, phrases or ideas are put forth in increasing order of importance. It adds to the overall effect of the piece.

For e.g. He came, he aced and he conquered. Focus on how his victory has been highlighted.

Solved Example of a Descriptive Writing Piece

Describe about a set of new clothes.

The monotony of wearing the same set of clothes was destroyed instantly when the new denim and the sunny yellow t-shirt beamed and looked forward to be kept prim and proper, in the left side of the cupboard.

The vibrant yellow, the stonewashed denim, the snow white full shirt and a crisp black cotton trouser were the new additions to my old sartorial family- Not a bouncy self, the denim always brushed the dolor off my spirit.

The white shirt though gave me chills of anxiety off my spine since I was a veteran at staining my clothes with ink or the most strangest of things such as food, colours, sometimes a random piece of mud etc.

This state of mind obviously meant to keep the snow white apparel as guarded as a princess and to absolutely overuse the other newbees as if I would never get a second chance to hone them.

The garish yellow, on the other hand, was as pleasant as the gentle sunlight of dawn beautifully caressing my spirit like never before. This piece of outfit was treated with lavish praise from my buddies and that seemed to add more cheer and joviality to it – an already beaming piece of cloth- Unexpectedly, the yellow tee and the white shirt were quite friendly with each other, hugging upclose in the narrow part of the attic. The crisp black trousers, however, were stringent and stoic, expecting to be ironed to perfection and to be mounted on a super similar black hanger, just about right in the centre of all the apparel. An alpha personality outfit-I must say.

Comments:
- [D100]: Strong vocabulary
- [D101]: Personification
- [D102]: Appropriate idiom
- [D103]: Visual Imagery to engage the reader
- [D104]: Catchy word usage
- [D105]: Personification and Hyperbole
- [D106]: Humour for more effect
- [D107]: Simile for effective comparison
- [D108]: Power vocabulary
- [D109]: Hyperbole and Personification
- [D110]: Humour and Punctuation (Single dash)
- [D111]: Vivid Imagery, Humour and Personification
- [D112]: Dramatic tone, very figurative and full of punches

On one of my cultural events, the classic white-black combination, my new fashion favourite, stood tall amidst other foppish folk who were flaunting too vibrant outfits with no avail.

As a student co-ordinator, my dress code completely ticked many boxes of being dapper, neat and relevant for the occasion.

With head held high(both the top and the bottom wear), I too ,felt a deep sense of pride and adulation for my new white glistening shirt and extremely smart black trouser who were both loyal servants to the cause of feeling special and getting venerated for the same.

These new set of clothes setup a fascinating, fresh, frolicky stance to my youth which was a bit bogged down because of too much of repetition in fashion as well as the same mono-coloured gear.

Some Key Adjectives for Descriptive writing

1. **Describing a person's physical appearance:**

   Fat- Chubby cheeks, Corpulent, Hefty, Brawny, Thewy, Sinewy, He-man

   Thin – Frail, Emaciated, Etiolated, Lanky

   Flushed – Florid, Blushing

   Pale – Lassitude, Enervated, Torpid

   Eyes- Twinkling, Bloodshot, Beady, Round as a sphere

2. **Describing a person's emotions :**

   Happy – Beaming, Sunny, Cheerful, Joyous, Ecstatic, Euphoric, In seventh heaven, On cloud nine, Sanguine

   Sad- Doleful, Dejected, Overwrought, Gloomy, Saturnine

   Energetic- Sprightly, Spirited, Vivacious, Peppy, Zealous

   Bitter- Sour, Turbid, Bilious, Splenetic, Harsh

3. **Describing nature:**

   Scenic, Lush, Verdant, Bucolic, Peaceful, Idyllic, Halcyon, Picturesque

CHAPTER 12

NARRATIVE WRITING

Narrative writing or fictional writing entails building stories with creative flair and originality that not only engage the reader but have a powerful impact, appeal and plot.

Fictional writing primarily necessitates having a well-connected plot, strong characters that are relatable and a proper structure so that the audience can properly and perfectly understand the arc of the story.

The inspirations of the stories can be realistic or based on life experiences or completely imaginative and fantastical. Accordingly, there are various genres of fiction:

1. Classical or Literary Fiction – Focuses on characters more than the plot.
2. Action and Adventure Fiction
3. Mystery and Crime Fiction
4. Speculative fiction – It can be sub categorised as:
   Fantasy
   Horror
   Science fiction
5. Romantic fiction
6. Coming of age fiction –Focus on the growth of the character from childhood to youth
   Bildungsroman – It can be sub classified under coming of age fiction and highlights the psychological and moral development.
7. Contemporary fiction
8. Comedy

Essential Elements of Narrative Writing in IGCSE

Narrative writing can be majorly, completely imaginative fiction or realistic fiction based on real life experiences where one can connect with the emotions better.

The story prompts asked in IGCSE are mostly realistic, based on real life experiences.

Despite it being narrative or a story retelling, it needs a proper structure and flow with a strong beginning, engaging middle and an impactful end.

The salient elements of narrative fiction are:

1. Engaging opening or introduction:

As any other writing, a story needs to have an engaging opening or introduction. This can be achieved by creating a rich setting in which the story takes place. A vivid description of the setting in terms of whether it is rural, urban, semi-urban, modern, ancient, fantastical sets the tone for the overall tale.

The key facets of a setting need to be described in-depth utilising layered sentences and evocative vocabulary, words that breathe the essence of the backdrop where all the events happen. Overall, a setting should enhance the plot.

E.g.

As a child in formative years, I distinctly remember my native place, Coorg, as being the most picturesque, coconut tree laden landscape with bouts of fresh air, aromatic earth and so many scenic places to visit. In stark contrast to a nature friendly abode, I am now stranded within the immeasurable smoke, soot and breathlessness of a typical city dwelling.

> **Commented [D113]:** It is a countryside setting, beautiful and drastically different from where the character lives.

2. Plot:

Plot is the spine of the story and includes all the key elements and happenings of the story and how the story is going to progress.

It is of utmost importance to decide the plot before writing the story in the examination so that it can be effectively developed.

In this case, the plot is about a girl, originally from Coorg but living in the busy metropolit of Mumbai. She has a deep desire to go back to her roots and help the villagers by providing them with better facilities like quality schools, hospital etc. When she goes back to her village, she faces lot of hostility from the conservative villagers and the story is about how she wins this challenging battle at the end.

3. Introduce and build the characters (effective characterisation):

After creating the setting and fixing the plot, it is paramount to introduce well developed characters, the central character or the protagonist as well as other characters. As a rule of thumb, in IGCSE exam, since the story is only about 350-450 words, it is ideal to just focus on 2-3 characters so that one can give justice to them too.

Let us see how this main character in this story comes about:

As I have mentioned innumerable times earlier that soul feels strangulated in a city, I am planning to relocate to Coorg for good. The whole anticipation of meeting my old friends, breathing the same old freshest air and having that sense of my abandon and disconfinement already fills my heart with real joy. Just two more days left! I go back to where I belong.

> **Commented [D114]:** The character loves nature and countryside
>
> **Commented [D115]:** She has a strong sense of freedom.

I, Trisha S, a bubbly, ambitious girl from Mumbai had Disneyland dreams from childhood. Unlike others who fancied being a renowned doctor or an Engineer (a typical Indian youth penchant), I wanted to be a social worker. Helping the needy just ticked all my boxes .That was the major motive of relocating to Coorg, a land of coffee, spices, interesting people but some harsh realities – inadequate access to education, remoteness defying progress and so on.

> **Commented [D116]:** Motive of the character

4. Introducing a conflict, challenge or an obstacle (rounded, layered and real)

The next step in carving a great story is to introduce a conflict, challenge or an obstacle in the plot to add to the drama and keep the audience hooked.

It can be done as follows in this story:

I had come here to Virajpet with noble intentions and oxygen high dreams to make a change. Is facilitating a change that easy? Had I forgotten the local chaos and the antagonism that it would kick start? How naïve I was to just imagine everything would sail smoothly! One sunny morning, I was just sitting in the verandah sipping on my hot ginger tea. To my absolute shock, three youngsters, with thick black moustaches and hefty body structure just barged into my house. It was not a very favourable sight to say the least. They threatened me in local language that if I start flying too much, they might cut my wings. To cut the long story short, very few people wanted progress and development in the village. They were hale and hearty with the mores and the typicalities of that area- to get married early, to just pursue farming, mainly coffee plantation and not mingle with other communities. At this instant, my city life filled with fumes seemed okay compared to this mental turmoil almost on a daily basis. But as they rightly say, 'What kills you makes you stronger'.

> **Commented [D117]:** Present the conflict or the issue to its fullest and with clarity.

5. Resolution of the conflict with the climax:

It is just not important to introduce a conflict or a challenge but also to show explicitly how the protagonist has resolved the conflict or challenge as follows:

Being troubled excessively by these goons, one fine evening, I decided to take a village meeting wherein I present myself and my real objectives to the true stakeholders. To my surprise, the villagers assented to chip in. With an exasperated voice, I said," Friends, I am not here to destroy your local traditions but to augment them with knowledge and opportunity. I am sure many of you would have dreamed about golden careers for your kids or just good schools, hospitals within the vicinity. Does that mean we are getting uprooted or losing our identity? Not really. So please rethink and let us create a change together, hand in hand."

> **Commented [D118]:** Convincing dialogues and using interesting words as well as realistic speech that can facilitate a better connect with the audience

> **Commented [D119]:** The protagonist appeals to the villagers to work together.

6. Impactful conclusion as well as lure the reader into the prospective continuation of the story:

Any story is incomplete without a powerful and relevant conclusion. Some of the conclusions are a definite closure to the story while others are cliff-hangers leaving the readers curious, shocked or interested.

Conclusion-

After fighting many battles, sometimes wounded, sometimes enervated, I finally made through the finish line. A new school project was already on the way and the local cabinet minister had paid a visit for prospective hospital establishment.

I think, the day I came to know about this, I felt like a centurion leader, who was finally victorious and could proudly assert, "I lost some but I won the critical ones."

> **Commented [D120]:** Ending on a very solid note with powerful sentences, some idioms or phrases that have the ability to linger in the reader's mind.

Tips for writing an excellent story in Cambridge IGCSE:

1. Using direct speech in the form of dialogues between the characters is the key to cooking an ideal story.

2. Use of figurative devices in the right places, junctures and amount really garnishes a narrative writing piece. For instance:

a. Hyperbole or exaggeration can be used to portray sadness, grief, sense of victory, importance of hard work and contribution.
   E.g.
   I burnt the midnight oil to crack the competition.
   When he met her lover, it felt like seventh heaven.
   The solitude of my home and my self was scarier than a dark, forbidden forest.

3. Varying sentence structures- Utilising few shorter sentences ,phrases, idioms, exclamatory sentences and rhetorical questions adds to the overall worth and reach of a narrative piece.

Narrative Writing

E.g.

I was numb – Shorter sentence.

They tried everything under the sun but failed miserably- Phrase.

He was the apple of her eye- Idiom.

Can we just choose to be dormant and not stand up against oppression?

4. Most of the tales are written in past tense although some are futuristic or in present tense too.

5. Vocabulary needs to be vivid, emotive and evoking a range of emotions. Use of sensory words appealing to all the five senses adds to the richness and depth of description and narration. The detailed description of what appealed to the sense of sight, hearing, smelling, tasting and sensing i.e., Imagery, should be efficaciously used.

E.g.

The sun was dazzling like the most glittering necklace- Visual Imagery

The smell of the earth was the biggest appetiser- Olfactory Imagery

The sweet and sour taste of the lemon added a different taste to the dish and the diners absolutely relished that- Gustatory Imagery

I felt a sense of deep chill and eerie silence after entering the room- Tactile or Kinesthetic Imagery

The thundering applause after the girl performed is a permanently etched memory- Auditory Imagery

6. Portrayal of a scene needs to be in-depth exploring the exact feelings, emotions, experiences .This aids to intensely connect with the reader.

As I entered my own room, this bleak evening, I sensed a deep chill running down my spine, literally shaking my poise and induced an inveterate sense of dread and insecurity. What had gone wrong in the day? Why was I bullied so much? Do I deserve this? These unending streak of questions were hovering over my brain trying to corrode it and vitiate my sanity.

> **Commented [D121]:** Evocative vocabulary
>
> **Commented [D122]:** Dramatic sentence with Tactile Imagery explaining how the character sensed or felt something
>
> **Commented [D123]:** Rhetorical Questions are a very powerful tool
>
> **Commented [D124]:** Use of Personification as a key figurative device

Using paragraph structure as in new paragraphs to denote new topics, happenings, time points, locations, characters or experiences.

7. The introduction and ending needs to be very impactful, convincing, unique and emotionally charging.

In a true sense, cooking a flawless story is like curating the most delicious recipe with the most apt ingredients in right proportions and balance.

Solved Example:

Write a story beginning with, "I was late ..." Write about 350-450 words. Up to 16 marks are available for the content and structure of your answer, and up to 24 marks for the style and accuracy of your writing.

I was late! It was my wedding day, certainly a 'D-Day', since I was replete with combination of butterflies in my stomach, anticipation and excitement. I had been awaiting this since I was a child. The sun was high in the sky-a perfect companion for a day that needed vigour and verve. I checked my phone to take one final look at the time.

> **Commented [D125]:** A dramatic and slightly humorous start is ideal.

My heart skipped a beat-13 missed calls, countless texts and the clock hands glaring at 1pm. My wedding was supposed to commence at 1.30 pm at the High Street Chapel. I was still stuck in the salon, getting merrily ready for the best day of my life. We were supposed to finish at 12.30 but as vanity goes, time is never enough for a girl to be in her best possible shoes.

> **Commented [D126]:** Keeping the audience engaged with impactful lines, humour and exaggeration.

How could I possibly be late for my own wedding? How nerve wracking and hilarious – a deadly duo!

> **Commented [D127]:** Use of rhetorical questions and exclamatory sentences add to the overall effect

I hadn't packed my bags either. I frantically rushed around my apartment. I set my phone down, afraid to check the messages. It started buzzing, I was getting a call from my dad. I didn't answer as I figured out that I could just come up with an excuse after getting there.

> **Commented [D128]:** Visual imagery

I began to pack my bags and the chore seemed timeless. It wasn't ending at all. I mean, how much did I really need for an afternoon? But, that is how it always is, isn't?

> **Commented [D129]:** A conversational tone, effective application of Hyperbole.

I had to strain desperately to get the bag closed. I had a final look in the sacred mirror reflecting not just the foundation but my joy too. I called a taxi, trembling. It was a catastrophe. The taxi also took its own time like me and lo behold! We reached the venue at 2 pm. That was outright 30 minutes late for a traditional Christian wedding.

> **Commented [D130]:** Keeping the high pulse drama mixed with well-crafted funny lines that just explain the whole chaos of delay.

To say the church was full of commotion and drama would be an understatement. My parents were literally on the verge of fainting, my bridegroom confused and devastated and the priest annoyed and disappointed.

Well, I had company of these strange emotions unlike the bridesmaids but I hanged on. Thirty minutes late or not, I got married and lived happily ever after.

> **Commented [D131]:** Conclusion that keeps you hooked

AUTHOR BIOGRAPHY:

A dentist researcher by qualification but a mentor-writer by passion and profession, Dr. Jyuthica.K. Laghate has wholeheartedly dedicated 18 years of her professional life to teaching English and Verbal Reasoning to students regionally, nationally and globally. Her body of work can be determined as preparing students for Cambridge IGCSE/ A levels English and English literature along with other GCSE boards as well as English for competitive exams such as GRE, GMAT, SAT and IELTS to guide them comprehensively at every step of their overseas education.

She is a celebrated educator and writer. Some of her accolades are: Nomination as a Best Author-Literature and Fiction by the Navi Mumbai Chamber of Business and Industries, Best Writing Style award by Ukiyoto and Best Inspirational fiction 2022 by Srgliterary awards for the book, 'The Empty Handed Altruist',High Teaching Quotient Mentor by the CENTA Hall of Fame, Best Overseas Education Mentor by India Education awards and National Rank at All India English Teaching Professionals Olympiad.

As a founder of one of its kind 'Guru Shishya' based Advanced English Knowledge Academy based on the unique 'Knowledge Café Teaching Philosophy' widely endorsed by stalwarts like Harvard

University, her main mission is to really enhance the English of students and make them proficient in all forms of English communication.

Writing became an innate element of the mission which initially started with publishing academic books on English vocabulary etc. The real her is about ruminating on the wonders of the universe, curiously researching abstract concepts such as link between spirituality and modern world, Indian Vedic culture and its application, body soul relationship and communication.

Along with academic writing, creative writing especially on abstract topics and spheres has been her passion. Through her books, she wants to spread the message of purity, clarity, innocence and power of now. Writing in her opinion is a tete'-e-tete' with the world but through written words and thoughts and mute reflections.

She believes her writing is an eclectic mix of the various interests and career experiences she draws and therefore is artistic yet scientific, abstract yet centred and humorous yet piercing....

Kind Regards,

Dr. Jyuthica.K. Laghate

Founder, Dr. J's Knowledge Café
Email: jyuths@gmail.com
Mobile: +917447789343

www.ingramcontent.com/pod-product-compliance
Lightning Source LLC
LaVergne TN
LVHW070539070526
838199LV00076B/6809